CHARITIES OF FRANCE.

CHARITIES OF FRANCE

IN 1866.

AN

ACCOUNT OF SOME OF THE PRINCIPAL EXISTING CHARITABLE INSTITUTIONS IN THAT COUNTRY.

"Dieu veut que nous portions le fardeau les uns des autres; celui des pauvres c'est sa misère, celui des riches c'est sa richesse." — St. Augustine.

NOT PUBLISHED.

BOSTON:
GOULD AND LINCOLN,
59 WASHINGTON STREET.
1867.

ROCKWELL AND ROLLINS, PRINTERS,
122 WASHINGTON STREET, BOSTON.

PREFACE.

THE information contained in the following pages respecting French charitable institutions may be of interest to those who are concerned in the management of kindred associations in this country.

For the facts obtained, the compiler has depended upon recently-published works and official documents.

He is indebted to Monsieur Armand Husson, Director of the General Administration of Public Charities in Paris, for valuable reports, as well as for a free pass to visit the various establishments under his charge.

BOSTON, *January*, 1867.

CONTENTS.

CHAPTER VIII.

CHAPTER IX.

CHAPTER X.

CHAPTER XI.

CHAPTER XII.

CHAPTER XIII.

CHAPTER XIV.

CHAPTER XV.

CHAPTER XVI.

CHAPTER XVII.

CHAPTER XVIII.

CHAPTER XIX.

CHAPTER XX.

CHAPTER XXI.

CHAPTER XXII.

CHAPTER XXIII.

CHAPTER XXIV.

CHAPTER XXV.

CHAPTER XXVI.

CHAPTER XXVII.

CHAPTER XXVIII.

CHAPTER XXIX.

CHAPTER XXX.

CHAPTER XXXI.

CHAPTER XXXII.

CHAPTER XXXIII.

CHAPTER XXXIV.

CHARITIES OF FRANCE.

CHAPTER I.

MODERN PARIS.

TRAVELLERS who visit Paris cannot fail to be impressed with the splendor of its public avenues and buildings, and the magnitude of the improvements now in the course of completion. Modern Paris can scarcely be recognized by one who visited it a quarter of a century ago, and the stranger is constantly impressed with the marks of energy and perseverance which have been able to transform the dark and narrow strets of the Latin quarter into broad avenues lined with stately buildings. The changes wrought in the external appearance of the populace is not less striking. The *Poissarde* of 1790 can hardly be found in the fish-market of 1866. The odorous and filthy den occupied by the virago of that day is transformed into an elegant structure of iron and glass. A respectable though talkative matron, in a neat white cap, retails her fish and lobsters from a pure white marble slab, behind which she is sitting, or, if you prefer it, transfers them all living from a tank of pure running water at her feet. There is perhaps no population, not excepting our own, where there is at the present time (1866) more evidence of thrift and well-being. Public reports and statistics show that there is much poverty; but we see little evidence of suffering; and the miserable, degraded, and half-naked beings everywhere seen in Great Britain can hardly be found in France, even in the poorest localities. The improvement in dress and cleanliness among the mechanics and laborers is very striking. It might not be safe to say that the character of the people has improved in the same degree with their material condition, for very recent events in European as well as in American history prove that the same incitements tend to the same results, and that the masses, when blinded by political frenzy, will still commit excesses as in former periods.

The cause of this general appearance of thrift and prosperity may be fairly ascribed to the long-continued peace, the general diffusion of education and intelligence among the people, and last, but not least, a more general sense of religious obligation and respect for the outward observances of the church. Personal observation as well as the universal testimony show that outward religious observances are more respected, and the public religious services of the church better attended, than for a long period of years. In 1831 the number of children in attendance on the primary schools was 1,935,624, or 1,200,715 boys and 734,909 girls. In 1846 the number had increased to 3,240,436, and in 1857 to 3,850,000. For the last nine years the increase has probably been in still greater proportion. Notwithstanding all these evidences of improvement and signs of prosperity, we know that large numbers receive public aid, and we are led to wonder why so little evidence of public misery is seen, and what are the instrumentalities by which such results are effected. The object of the following pages is to furnish information in regard to some of these after giving a brief historical sketch of public charitable effort, or, as it is technically called, "Bienfaisance Publique,"* in France during past centuries.

* The term *Bienfaisance*, signifying a virtue emanating from the love of our kind, was first introduced into the French language in 1725, by the Abbé de St. Pierre. He says: "Since I have seen Christians dishonor the term of charity by the persecution of their enemies, and heretics profess to practise Christian charity by persecuting other heretics, or even Christians, I have sought for a word which exactly expressed the idea of doing good to others, and I have found none more suitable than the word Bienfaisance. Let those who will, use it. At any rate, it expresses my meaning, and cannot be misunderstoood."

CHAPTER II.

HISTORY OF ANCIENT SYSTEMS OF RELIEF.

IN early times the bishops and clergy were the only dispensers of alms to the poor. The first council of Orleans, held during the reign of Clovis, in the year 511, ordained that the whole income of the church should be devoted to the maintenance of public worship, the support of the clergy and the poor, and the ransom of captives. A later council, held in the same city in 549, ordained that criminals should be visited in the prisons every Sunday, by the archdeacon and provost, who should supply their wants at the expense of the church, and further, that the bishops should take particular care of the lepers. The council of Tours, held in 566, denounces as murderers of the poor, al who shall appropriate to their own use the property of the church; and if they persist in their evil courses, "after three warnings, we will all assemble, and in concert with our bishops, priests, and clergy, since we have no other arms, we will proclaim from the choir of the church, against such murderers, the 108th Psalm, to draw upon them the malediction of Judas, that they may die not only excommunicated, but accursed."

The second council of Macon, held in 585, ordained that "The bishops should recommend to all the virtue of hospitality; and to enable them better to practise it themselves, they should harbor no dogs in their houses, lest access thereto should be less free to the poor." The synod of Auxerre soon afterwards recommended to the faithful, in order that their devotions should be more acceptable, that they should make gifts to those poor persons whose names should be registered in the church records.

In the year 549, the council of Orleans confirmed the establishment of a hospital at Lyons, founded by Childebert and his queen. Before the end of the same century, Paris had established the Hospital of St. Julien Le Pauvre, and Reims and Auterre each possessed a similar institution. Before the close of the next century nearly every considerable town had its hospital, while Paris possessed several. As early as the reign of Charlemagne they were classified for the reception of five kinds of inmates, — the poor, the sick, the orphans, the aged, and children. To meet the large expenditures required for the relief of the poor, the ransom of captives, and the support of hospitals, the clergy received vast benefices. Following the example of Constantine and his successors, the Merovingian kings were most liberal in their grants to the clergy. Clovis, for instance, gave to the church at Reims as much land as St. Remy could ride around during the royal nap at noon, and this grant was made in accordance with the prayer of the inhabitants, who preferred to be vassals to the church rather than to the king. Childebert and his Queen Ulthugoth, as before stated, built and endowed the hospital at Lyons, and their example was followed by their subjects, who conferred large sums in public charity.

From the reign of Pepin in 752, the first of the second or Carlovingian race of kings, the clergy ceased to be the exclusive almoners to the poor. Under Charlemagne, in 809, the following became the law of the kingdom:

"The counts must take care of the poor; each must feed his own poor. Let no one despoil the poor of the little which remains to him. The widow, the orphan, and the helpless, are placed under the protection of the king, as they *are* under God. They should enjoy legal peace, and the cause in which they are interested should be judged with especial care and diligence. Advocates should be given to the poor to prevent oppression and deception by the rich. To insure the execution of these charitable measures, *missi dominici*, charged with full powers, will go forth, and visit all parts of this vast empire."

Notwithstanding these enactments, the church continued to be the source from whence flowed the streams of public charity, and Charlemagne himself was prodigal in his gifts. During the wars and confusion which followed the death of that monarch, all organized institutions for the relief of the poor had nearly disappeared. On the approach of the year 1000, which in the popular mind was fixed upon as heralding the end of the world, and to be preceded by wars, famine, and the prevalence of the *feu sacré* or St. Anthony's fire large sums were bestowed in public charity, while wills and deeds in favor of hospitals and other charitable institutions were headed by the inscription, "*Adventante mundi vespero*." With the crusaders came the diseases incident to large armies thrown upon a foreign shore without commissariat or discipline, and exposed to the vicissitudes of climate, and the pangs of hunger and thirst. The principal diseases thus brought were the leprosy and scurvy, and scarcely a town or village was without some kind of hospital or refuge for patients afflicted with the disorder first named. In the twelfth century, according to official statements, no less than nineteen thousand hospitals and retreats were opened in Europe for lepers. With the increase of these establishments came abuses in the administration of funds, and consequent edicts in favor of reform from the councils of Paris held in 1212, and from those of Arles and Ravenna held during the same century. Upon the complaint of Durant, Bishop of Mende, the council of Vienne, held in 1312, appointed laymen to aid in managing the hospitals and public establishments, and adopted a constitution for their government, called Clementine, in honor of Clement V., who presided over the council. It does not appear that the poor gained by the change of organization, as frequent edicts to check flagrant abuses are found during following centuries.

In a royal edict dated at Fontainebleau, December 15, 1543, we read:

"As we have been informed of the great disorders which exist in the lazarettoes and leproseries founded during past ages in our realm by our predecessors, kings, dukes, counts, and other seigneurs, as well as by many other devoted and faithful Christians, cities, chapters, and religious communities, of which the funds have been perverted, the title-deeds and charters lost or stolen by the administrators and governors of the same, who persecute and strangle the sick poor and lepers, and otherwise treat them so cruelly that they are compelled to quit the place and beg through the surrounding towns and villages, and besides do in other ways misapply the revenues, goods, and inheritances of the said hospitals, bequeathing them to their children, relatives, and friends, and other enormous abuses; now, therefore, I give to the bailiffs, seneschals, and judges, the supervision of the said hospitals and lazarettoes, with power to remove the said administrators."

These measures having been found insufficient, Francis I. in 1544 established the "*Bureau Generale des Pauvres,*" which was charged with the duty of levying an annual tax, called "*tax d'aumone,*" or poor-tax, on all princes, lords, towns, and landholders.

An edict of Henry II., dated in 1547, ordains that—

"Each inhabitant of Paris shall pay a special tax to meet the wants of the poor. But the weekly collections and gifts received in each parish for the relief of the poor, almost innumerable in Paris, are so much diminished, and come in most part from persons in easy circumstances, burghers, and inhabitants of our now cold-hearted city, and it being inconvenient and impossible to continue longer the distribution of alms to the said poor, which have hitherto been weekly distributed, — a matter which causes us great regret and displeasure, — Parliament shall appoint commissioners who shall receive the alms and gifts which all liberally-disposed persons shall be inclined to give."

By an edict dated in 1553, the general supervision of all the hospitals in the kingdom was given to the grand almoner of France. A few years later Charles IX. authorized the appointment of a joint commission of the clergy and laity to administer the public charitable funds. The gradually increasing influence of the laity in the administration of public affairs, as will be seen by reference to past legislation, is strikingly shown by the act of Henry III., in which it was provided, "That no one shall hereafter be commissioned as administrator for the government of the goods and revenues of the lazarettoes and hospitals, other than simple burghers, tradesmen, and laborers, and not ecclesiastics, gentlemen, archers, public officials, their followers, or persons by them introduced."

CHAPTER III.

SYSTEM OF RELIEF FROM 1599 TO 1788.

BY an edict dated in 1599, Henry IV. established a "*Chambre de Charité Chretienne*," and Louis XIII., in 1612, created a board entitled, "*Chambre Generale de Reformation.*" Thus far public efforts for the relief of the poor had been directed to the establishment of arge buildings or groups of buildings, where the sick and the well, the vagrant and the idle, had been herded together without regard to age, circumstances, or sex. Under the influence of the legislation just quoted, a better system was inaugurated for the relief of the destitute at their own dwellings, — a system which had been approved as far back as the reigns of Charlemagne and Saint Louis, but which had never been put in practice until the times of Francis I. and Henry II. The first of these kings, in 1536, ordered that "poor invalids, who have chambers, lodgings, or other refuge, should be fed and cared for at their own dwellings;" and whatever may have been his merits in other respects, he, perhaps, may be entitled to the credit of having established the Dispensary system, which has only been perfected during the present century, and has proved to be of incalculable benefit, in an economical and moral point of view. In the reign of Henry II. several work-shops were established in Paris for "*healthy vagabonds*," and it was arranged that "poor and helpless invalids, who have houses, chambers, or other lodgings, in the city or suburbs, should receive reasonable aid at their own dwellings, or other convenient place. The poor and helpless who cannot work and have no houses, chambers, or place of shelter, shall be promptly conducted to the hospitals, hotels, or Maisons Dieu. Curates, vicars, and wardens, shall keep an exact record of the poor in their respective parishes. Paupers who have received aid, and who shall be found begging in the city, shall be punished; *adults with the whip, and little children with the rod*." In 1642 a "*Bureau des Pauvres*," consisting of clergy, church-wardens, and prominent citizens, was established; but from contemporary documents it would appear that the system of domiciliary aid was but partially carried out. An official report states that "they gave much and they gave unwisely," and the matter ended by resorting to the old plan of sending the poor to the public hospitals. Street-begging had now become an intolerable evil, in spite of the many stringent measures taken to suppress it. Paris was infested by an army of forty thousand beggars, called, in the language of the time, *truands*, *pietres*, *maligneux*, who formed a community by themselves. They acknowledged neither the claims of law nor religion, and plundered the citizens without scruple whenever the opportunity was offered. The evil became so intolerable that stringent measures were decided upon, and in 1657 the beggars were summoned to appear, between the 7th and 13th of May, in the court of the Hospital de la Pitié, in order that they might be registered, and distributed among the various public establishments. Five thousand only appeared in answer to the call, but for a time a great improvement was manifest in the capital. A contemporary writer says that "the greater portion of the beggars left for the provinces, and the most sensible of them managed to gain a subsistence without begging, while the most infirm invalids were transformed by their own proper will." They, however, soon reappeared, and in 1659, encouraged by the archers of the guard, who had taken them under their protection, made several attacks upon the soldiers guarding one of the hospitals. The thirty years' war, with the confiscation of the property of the clergy and religious houses, and the prodigality of Louis XIII. and Louis XIV., reduced an immense number of persons to poverty, and beggary increased in proportion. By an edict of 1656, Louis XIV. concentrated under one administration, known as the Hôpital Generale, the five public establishments in Paris, viz., La Pitié, Le Refuge, Le Scipion, Le Bicetre, and La Savouniere, all of which were used indiscriminately for the reception of the sick and paupers. The directors were appointed for life, and were entrusted with the entire charge of the paupers of Paris, with full powers to punish the contumacious, to make collections in their behalf, and to place charity-boxes in the churches, public squares, shops of tradesmen, or in any other place where the people could be excited to charitable effort. They were also permitted to receive gifts and legacies, and to manage all the goods, real and personal, belonging to the hospitals, without accounting to other authority. The clergy having the spiritual care of the inmates in what a writer calls "this immense Versailles of misery," found themselves entirely subjected to the rule of the directors. An order was issued that a hospital on the same plan should be established in every large city and town in the kingdom. Stringent laws were enacted against street-beggary; amongst others the following: "All persons are forbidden to give alms to beggars in the streets or public places, — no motives of compassion, pressing necessity, or other necessity notwithstanding, — under penalty of a fine of six livres. Landlords are also forbidden to harbor or lodge beggars on their premises."

This experiment of Louis XIV. proved a failure, from the abuse of the inordinate powers given to the directors, or, as a writer has said, "he did not leave a drop less in the sea of pauperism which he had attempted to dry up." Little was done in this direction by Louis XV.

In 1781 the Emperor Joseph, who had interested himself particularly in the subject of charitable economy, paid a visit to his brother-in-law, Louis XVI., and after an inspection of the Hotel Dieu, made earnest remonstrances in regard to the horrible condition of that institution. Louis directed Poyet, architect of the Hotel Dieu, to investigate the subject, and in 1785 the report was submitted by the king to the Academy of Sciences, where it was fully discussed, and a committee appointed on the subject, consisting of the following members: Lassove, Tenon, Tillet, Darcet, Daubenton, Coulomb, La Place, Lavoisier, and Bailly. Francis Arago says of this committee, "In no age, in no country, could there be gathered more knowledge or more virtue." On application of the committee for admission to the Hotel Dieu, they were met with a flat refusal by the directors, and it was only by an express order from the king that they were enabled to enter the hospital. The report of the commission was drawn up by Mons. Bailly, and from it we take the following extracts:

"The committee have seen the convalescents occupying the same wards with the sick, the dying with the dead. They also found the wards of the insane contiguous to those of patients who had submitted to severe operations, and who could obtain no sleep on account of the frantic cries which the former kept up day and night. The ward St. Joseph is devoted to pregnant women, the virtuous and the vile. Three or four may be found in one bed, exposed to contagion, and with the risk of injury to their infants. Four or five women, who had been confined at different periods, were found huddled in one bed. The mind revolts at such a situation, in which they cannot fail to infect each other. The greater part perish, or leave the hospital in a dying condition. Each ward has several straw beds, for the dying, and for those whose beds are unfit for use. There, amidst the dying and the filthy, are often deposited those new comers who arrive early in the day, and have no place assigned them. The operating-room, in which the surgeons trepan, cut for stone, and amputate, contains at the same time those who are undergoing operations, as well as patients who have undergone, or are waiting for them. The work is done in the middle of the hall, where you can see the preparations as well as hear the cries of the poor wretches. Those whose turn is to come have presented to them what they are to suffer; and one can easily imagine the effect such a scene must have upon those who have already undergone the trial. The patient undergoes all the terrors and shocks, in addition to the dangers from inflammation and suppuration, which fearfully increase the hazards to life."

The report adds:

"The itch is almost universal at the Hotel Dieu. The surgeons, the Sisters of Charity, and the attendants, contract the disease directly from the patients or from their clothing. Patients leaving the hospital carry it home to their families; and thus the Hotel Dieu is an inexhaustible source from which the disease is spread throughout Paris."

Further investigations showed that equally great abuses prevailed in other institutions. At the Bicetre, which was devoted to the treatment of venereal diseases, twenty-five beds were occupied by two hundred patients, and two-thirds of the number died. As a moral lesson, every patient was whipped on his entrance as well as on his departure, and yet, during the year, there were many more applications than admissions. At the Salpetriere, in 1788, there were eight thousand inmates at one time crowded together.

CHAPTER IV.

MODERN LEGISLATION.

AMONG the various questions of social economy, about which there are so many conflicting opinions in France at the present day, no one, perhaps, has received more careful consideration than the administration of the public funds for the relief of the poor. In every age of French history this subject has been a leading one in the mind of government, and has been accompanied by legislation corresponding to the public intelligence and morals. This was particularly the case about the close of the last century, when the solicitude of statesmen was seriously aroused, and long and earnest debates ensued in the Legislative Assembly. Great differences of opinion were entertained by eminent and learned authorities, and numerous publications were issued, many of them the result of learned and careful investigation. Amidst the throes of revolution, when all established principles seemed to be shaken, and everything was questioned, the public obligations towards the poor who had been reduced to poverty by the effects of war and general disorder, became a subject of paramount interest and necessity. The question was, Whether the ancient charitable foundations be maintained on their old basis, or should they be given up, and a new experiment tried, more in accordance with the supposed light of the age? The reformers, hostile to past precedents and strong in numbers, were in favor of the latter plan, while those who were willing to be governed by the light of past experience advocated the maintenance of the old system, with such amendments as might be called for by the new order of things.

Daunou, whose patriotism and moderation are well known, exclaimed in Convention, "If it is so hard to create, how can we make up our minds to destroy? After ten years of revolution, should it not be pardonable to feel how precious is a thing which exists? Can we be tempted to throw down that which only needs slight modification, to build in its place, with painful and fruitless efforts, a new edifice, of which it will be easier to trace the plan than to find the materials?"

These moderate counsels found but little favor in a body bent upon innovations; but before deciding upon any new plan of organization, it was found necessary to appoint a committee to investigate the causes of the public distress. The more serious the wound, the greater need was there that its depth should be probed. Several works, published by well-known and esteemed authors, threw much light upon the subject, and revealed the true causes of the disorder. Each, according to his peculiar opinions, proposed the proper mode of remedy. Some, philosophers, but above all Christians, regarded the subject of public aid to the poor in a charitable point of view, and their relief as a public duty. Others, statesmen, far-seeing and rigid economists, considered the subject mainly in its necessary connection with social organization, and the obligations of government. Others, more recent writers, viewing the matter in a merely political light, rejecting former principles, have sought to revive the theories of the revolutionary epoch, which are as dangerous as they are impracticable, and as such have not survived the light of public discussion. Without entering into the details respecting the various opinions of the writers, we find that the almost unanimous opinion of those best able to judge of subjects relating to public charity, is, that the principal, if not the sole cause of the public distress among the lower classes of society in France, is the want of moral and intellectual culture, on account of which the laborer is destitute of the intelligence necessary to guide him in the difficult circumstances of his career, or to acquire that kind of prudence and self-respect which can alone enable him to meet them. At this point the harmony of opinion ceases; for however unanimous in recognizing the greatness of the evil, those minds so acute in discussing it and its causes differ entirely as to the proper remedy. All seem to recognize the end to be attained, but differ as to the means of reaching it. One of the most esteemed of the writers alluded to says:

"Owing to the number and the diversity of the works which have been published on public charity, there has arisen a difference of opinion and clashing of systems, which have confused some, and have filled the minds of others with the discouragement of skepticism. The art of public charity (*bienfaisance*), which at first sight appears so simple, and so easy in its applications, has raised the most difficult problems. Even the foundations of the social organization have been questioned. Some have maintained the right of the poor to a support as sacred, and have imposed the obligation on society as a debt, while others have considered such a system as a perversion of true charity, and the source of pauperism. Light has been thrown upon the subject since 1839. The opinions advanced during the Revolution of 1848 have been useful, in that they have excited public notice, and have occupied the attention of some of the ablest minds."

Mr. Thiers, in the report of a committee of the Legislative Assembly, says:

"That which the old order of society has left us to do, is just that which is doubtful, problematical, debatable, and for that reason is left to be done.

"Although some of the untried experiments are the most doubtful, it does not follow that they are to be condemned, or that in former times everything had been thought of and perfected, leaving us nothing to do. Although much good was formerly done, there remains much to do, but it is not the good which we dream of, or imagine. In this, as in everything else, the State (which is no other than man himself) is shut up in the narrow limits of the possible, and to promise to do more is not doing it. It is making an idle engagement, and raising hopes which disappoint and often bring despair."

The same writer says, in another place:

"Nothing has been completed, and we predict to all ages, that no one will have the honor of completing the work."

The opinions of Mr. Thiers should have the more weight, as, for eleven years, he presided over the most extensive charitable administration in Europe. From his official relations he was, perhaps, better qualified than any one else to give advice as to the relief of poverty in large communities, and to recognize the fact, that the actual benefits obtained are not so much in the proportion of the sums provided, as in their careful and wise distribution. If experience has taught anything, it is the fact, that the greater the amount given, the more do the wants increase. For this reason, it is essential to guard against those exaggerated sentiments of humanity which only tend to increase the evil which we are contending against. In whatever light we regard the system of public relief, — whether in its principles, its designs, or its results, — we must not fall into the error of believing that by increasing the amount of aid we shall ever satisfy the wants of poverty. At the same time, while we reason thus, we cannot abandon the poor man to his fate, in refusing him all participation in the benefactions which an enlightened charity should bestow.

CHAPTER V.

PLANS OF RELIEF DURING THE REVOLUTION.

IN the year 1789, the population of France was about 25,-000,000, divided into three orders, — the clergy, the nobility, and the third estate or bulk of the nation. The clergy numbered 140,000, and possessed real estate to the value of 4,000,000,000 of livres, besides enjoying tithes valued at 80,000,000, and other perquisites. The second order, or nobility, were 80,000 in number, and owned about half the territory, and, like the clergy, were absolved from great public burdens by the State. The third estate, numbering 24,800,000, after paying tithes, feudal taxes, the support of the royal family and the court, was obliged to bear the cost of the army, navy, and general administration. These inequalities of taxation, added to the prodigalities of past reigns, brought on a financial crisis, accompanied by great misery and destitution among the lower orders, when the States General were convened in May, 1789. At this time, as is shown by official documents, there were 2,185 hospitals, containing 105,000 inmates. These were classed as follows:

For foundlings, 40,000; for sick, 25,000; infirm and aged, 49,000. Besides these, there were numerous depots for paupers, to say nothing of private charitable establishments.

The accommodation afforded by these institutions fell far short of the demand caused by the general distress. The depots for paupers had, between the years 1768 and 1790, received 230,000 persons, one-sixth of whom, or 45,000, had died. The expenses for the support of the same had been 29,700,000 livres; as Monsieur L'Ainé, a minister of Louis XVIII., in a report in the year 1818, says, "a horrible result in expense and mortality."

On the 21st of March, 1790, the National Assembly, "penetrated with the *eternal* truth, that the duty of providing for the subsistence of the poor in the construction of an empire is not less sacred than that of securing the prosperity of the rich," appointed a committee to take into consideration the whole subject of public charity, and the various plans of relief. This committee, of which the Duke of Rochefaucault was chairman, considered the subjects very fully, and submitted the results of their deliberations in a series of seven reports to the Assembly. After the assertion "that pauperism is not an offence, excepting for him who prefers it to honest labor," the committee concluded thus: "Society should aid without requiring labor from those who are incapacitated by age or infirmity. Every man has a right to his subsistence. The relief of indigence is a debt due by the State."

To determine, as nearly as possible, the number of poor having a right to public aid, the committee considered that the great mass of paupers could be divided into two classes, viz., one half, able-bodied, requiring help only during seasons of forced idleness from want of work, or accidental poor; the other half, confirmed paupers, consisting of the aged, the infirm, and children; while in the two classes there might be 50,000 sick. The estimated cost of relief was as follows:

For 50,000 sick, at 12 to 15 sous each per day,	12,000,000	livres.
For 500,000 aged, infirm, and children, at 50 or 60 livres each,	27,500,000	"
Cost of giving aid by employment of healthy poor, at rate of 60,000 livres in each department,	5,000,000	"
For suppression of beggars, for houses of correction, and cost of transportation,	3,000,000	"
Reserve fund, and expenses of administration,	4,000,000	"
	51,500,000	"

The 51,500,000 livres were to be raised annually by taxation, or were to form a part of the national obligation, and thereby pauperism was to be eradicated and ample means secured for the relief of the indigent. To secure the funds necessary for carrying out this reform, the committee proposed that the hospitals and public charitable establishments should be sold, and the proceeds be amalgamated with the property of the State. The measures recommended were never carried into effect, and although there was much legislation, the Republic left pauperism very much as it had been, until Napoleon, who took Louis XIV. for his model, grappled with the subject, and, as a writer informs us, "attached great importance and a great idea of glory to the destruction of mendicity, and like that king, also, he sought to accomplish it by concentrating and adding constantly to his own absolute powers. But in spite of his omnipotence, and perhaps on account of that omnipotence, he succeeded no better than Louis had done before him. The beggars mocked the man who mocked kings, and Napoleon was not able to leave as he wished this mark of his passage. He is gone, and beggary remains." The following are the words of Napoleon, written November 14th, 1807:

"I attach a great importance and a great idea of glory to the plan of destroying mendicity; the means are not wanting, but it seems to me that everything moves slowly, and yet the years go by. We must not live here in this world without leaving traces which shall make us to be remembered by posterity. I am about to depart for a month; you must manage by the 15th of December to have investigated all the details pertaining to this subject, so that, by a general desire, we can give the last blow to mendicity."

Whatever desirable results the emperor failed to accomplish, he effected a great object in removing from the statute-book the act by which the Republic had declared the right of the poor to public aid. He also recognized the obligation of the nation to make up any deficiency caused by expenditures by hospitals and almshouses for the relief of inmates.

CHAPTER VI.

COMPARATIVE MERITS OF HOSPITAL AND DISPENSARY SYSTEMS.

AMONG the discussions which arose during the civil dissensions in France, was that regarding the relative merits of the two systems of relief to the sick poor, viz., that afforded in public hospitals, and that given at their own dwellings, constituting what is now known as the dispensary system. Necker, in his work on the administration of the finances, says:

"Many persons question whether hospitals are a benefit to society, and the objection which they make is, that they foster idleness among the poor by removing the necessity for saving in order to secure themselves against the time of sickness and old age. It is true, that the hope of receiving aid in sickness, or a shelter in old age, might tend to make people less industrious and careful; but the wages of this class in France are so small, that it would be a hard and constant effort to save enough from their pittance to be of any service as a reserve fund. Nothing can be more conformed to the ideas of equity than these public establishments, where the worthy poor man finds relief in time of infirmity and sickness; and if there are times when the thought of such relief tends to make him less careful, there are other times when such reliance tends to preserve him from utter despair. We must, then, I think, adhere to the old notions of humanity, which time and the public sentiment of all countries have rendered sacred."

Other writers have urged the total abolition of public hospitals, and the treatment of the sick at home. Under this arrangement, all the public establishments for the sick were to be sold, thereby increasing the public revenue.* On the other hand, there would, say they, be a large saving of expense in the cost of furnishing, support, etc., and the sick could be cared for by contracts at fixed prices, "and would make the most of their meat and soup, and would warm themselves by the fires allowed them to make their *tisanes*" (herb drinks).

Amidst these discussions, at the request of the administrators and physicians of the Hotel Dieu, at Paris, a commission was appointed to consider the subject of the transfer of that institution to another locality, and its reorganization on a larger and improved plan. This committee, which has already been alluded to, consisted of Messrs. Lassove, Daubenton, Tenon, Bailly, Lavoisier, La Place, Coulomb, and Darcet. In discussing the arguments which had been proposed by the opponents of hospitals, they say:

" How can you be certain that the food and medicines furnished by the contractors are actually used by the sick, and that nothing is taken from them? If a price is paid for the care of the sick,

* According to Necker, there were in France, in 1789, 870 hospitals and hospices. In 1833, there were 1,329. In 1853, there were 1,324. From 1833 to 1852, a period of 20 years, 11,023,177 patients or inmates were received, making an annual average of 551,159. The mortality of the institutions in Paris has sensibly diminished since the last century. From 1724 to 1763, it carried from 22 to 26 per ct.; while from 1833 to 1852, leaving out the year 1849, when the cholera prevailed, the mortality varied from 8.67 to 8.85. There are now 20 medical schools attached to hospitals, with courses of lectures on *accouchements*.

and this price is to depend on the person or the nature of the disease, who is to make the classification? or should the price be the same for all, without distinction of age or sex, then it would be too large for one, and too little for another. And then it would not be possible to treat the sick thus, unless they have a home, and this many of them do not have. They have a room in common with others, or dark and unhealthy cellars, where they cannot remain in sickness. Must there not be hospitals for these unfortunate persons, whose sufferings are aggravated by their poverty?"

The anonymous author of a pamphlet published at the same period writes:

"It would not be safe to give the sick entirely up to the care of the attendants, who carry their food and medicines to them in their attics. It would be necessary to have some sort of direction, like that of a hospital, with this difference, that it would be movable instead of stationary, extended over a great field instead of being under the eye, and more extended because it would be necessary to increase the number of employées to look after the four or five thousand sick scattered over the city instead of being gathered into hospitals. The expenses of the administration would not thus be diminished. Furnishing by wholesale would cost less than by retail, and transporting supplies from place to place would increase the expense. A sick patient would not, sometimes, get the most simple medicine, unless it were brought from the other end of the town; every errand costs labor, and labor costs money. Some of the sick have neither relatives nor friends; others, perhaps, have a family, but its members are at work earning their own bread. Can they give up their own time to watch with and help the invalid? To do so, they must give up work, and thus would go to swell the ranks of the needy."

CHAPTER VII.

HOSPITALS AND HOSPICES. — TOLERATION THEREIN.

THE origin of hospitals dates far back, though the records of ancient nations furnish no account of any institutions like those of the present day.* We are indebted to Christianity — whose fundamental principle is charity — for this institution, which for many ages has had its opponents, and yet, in all civilized nations, has long been consecrated by the blessings of the poor. For many centuries the clergy were almost the only possessors of knowledge, and had the sole charge of the lower orders when suffering from sickness and the many evils to which they were exposed by the rapacity or cruelty of their landlords. On this account hospitals were formerly placed at the side of or near the convents, and the religious orders of both sexes considered it a meritorious work to care for the sick inmates. Most of the ancient establishments now in existence date their founda-

* A hospital is a place to receive the sick, while the hospice is destined to receive the aged, the infirm, and deserted children. In some of the French towns, the two terms are used indiscriminately, because the two institutions are placed under the same roof. The Latin word *hospitium*, from which the two words are derived, did not possess the same significance. The Romans had only their domestic infirmaries (*valetudineria*), principally for the cure of their slaves. The expressions *hospitium privatum, hospitium publiceum*, referred to hospitality in general, as exercised between individuals or nations.

tion from the time of the Crusades. We are told that the ancient knights, before entering upon perilous enterprises, sought to propitiate Heaven and atone for sins by largesses to the church, and by the establishment of hospitals for the poor, as well as for pilgrims and returning Crusaders.

Even at an earlier date, there existed in France several hospitals called *Maisons Dieu*, or *Hotels Dieu*, where the bishops and clergy received the sick and disabled poor. The principal of these was the Hotel Dieu, at Paris, whose foundation is ascribed to St. Landry, bishop of that city in the seventh century. Several were founded during the reigns of Charlemagne and St. Louis. A list of the principal hospitals and hospices is given in the following pages. The report of the committee for remodelling the Hotel Dieu led to the improvements which characterize the present hospital system, and to the removal of the various classes of patients, such as lying-in women, children, and persons affected with skin diseases, to special institutions.

There is so much similarity in plan and government of hospitals in the great cities of Europe and America, that it is hardly necessary to give minute details respecting such institutions in France. It may be well, however, to give a brief statement of the toleration exercised at the present day in regard to religion and systems of medical treatment. The information given is taken from recently-published authority. A late director of the administration writes as follows:

"There is one principle which has, at all times, governed the action of the administration of hospitals, and which, it seems to me, should be of general application. It is, that the physician should follow the dictates of his own conscience. He should be left entirely free in the choice as well as in the application of his remedies, and, at the same time, should be held responsible for the result of his prescriptions, the same as for his other acts as a physician. It was on the strength of this principle, constituting the only safe ground of the administration in such matters, that it tolerated a medical service in one of the hospitals of Paris, conducted by one who had renounced the doctrines which he had until then professed, and who took upon himself the responsibility of treating his patients by the method called homœopathic. All that the administration could do under these circumstances was to inquire from the statistics respecting the danger or the harmlessness of this method of treatment. Now, it was demonstrated, by tables prepared during the space of two years in the different wards of the hospital, that the mortality, so far from being greater in the ward of the physician alluded to, was less by about one-tenth than in the other wards.*

"In presence of the facts, the administration could not interfere without the risk of raising the cry of persecution; and all history shows that persecution has only served to make its subjects more prominent, and to confirm them in their doctrines. For the sake, then, of the distinguished defenders of allopathic medicine, would it have been wise to give their opponents the advantage of being considered victims by public opinion? Was it not the part of wisdom to leave all to the future, and insure the triumph of reason

* But it may be objected, that the homœopathic physician takes great care to admit to his ward only patients suffering from slight affections; that is to say, those who have the best chance of recovery, and can thus turn the scale in his favor. The administration replies, that this is only an assumption: that it can only consider facts, and that the facts given were authentic, and as such had indisputable authority, and should be sufficient to satisfy its conscience.

and truth? Such were the principles which actuated the administration in this matter, and which induced it to tolerate, in one of the hospitals, a system which it could not prohibit without encroaching upon the independence of the medical profession. Further than this, the physician who practised this system has since died, and the medical service of which he was the head has been restored to its former position."

The same liberality is shown in all matters pertaining to the religious services and instruction in the hospitals. Each hospital, according to size, has one or more Catholic almoners attached to it, who are appointed by the bishop of the diocese. It is their duty to administer gratuitously religious consolation and the sacrament, to facilitate patients in the performance of their religious duties, to perform divine service, to aid poor families by means of small grants, and to pay the last tribute of respect to the deceased. Ministers of denominations recognized by the government may be admitted by the administration to administer to patients of their respective churches. As the unrestricted admission of these ministers of different creeds might lead to differences and embarrassments, efforts at proselytism are strictly forbidden:

"If a patient belonging to a certain communion wishes to consult a minister of a different creed than that to which he belongs, the minister thus called should notify the superintendent, who will satisfy himself that it is done by his own free will. No stranger, whether a clergyman or layman, shall be allowed to perform any ministerial act, either preaching or religious rite.* The officers

* The salary of an almoner of the first class in a hospital is 2,000 francs with board and lodging. An assistant receives 700 francs. The ad-

of the institution will see that no inmate is forced to practise any religious rites or listen to any teaching which he shall declare to be repugnant. They should use every effort to promote harmony and good-will between the ministers themselves and ministers and members of the administration, as well as between all persons professing different sentiments. Every inmate shall have the privilege of bringing with him the books which are used in his denomination, or which are in accordance with his own personal belief; but no books shall be distributed, unless they be declared, and such distribution made under the sanction of the ecclesiastical authority by which such distribution is permitted. The general policy of the administration on the subject of religious ministrations in the hospitals, is set forth in a circular issued in 1854."

"The charity which watches at the door of the hospital, makes no inquiry as to the religious belief of the unfortunate patients who are admitted. Their sufferings and misfortunes are their only claims for relief; but when once admitted, besides the treatment for their recovery, to kind care and attention should be added the consolations of religion, which tranquillize the mind, inspire resignation in the hearts of the greatest sufferers, and give hope to the discouraged. Without imposing them upon any one, they should be within the reach of all. The Protestant and the Jew should see and hear the minister of his communion. The Catholic, always in the majority, should find on the premises a chapel in which to offer up his prayers, and a clergyman to visit and aid him in the performance of his religious duties. This happy religious influence should be exerted upon all, upon the convalescent as well as the

ministration gives no control or submission to ministers of any denomination, but declares that they shall be entitled to the greatest respect and protection from the authorities, as well as deference in all that concerns their proper functions.

dying, and after death the ceremonies of religion should be performed over every coffin. Such are the duties of the administration towards the sufferers committed to its care, and such is the mission of the ecclesiastic associated in this holy work."

CHAPTER VIII.

HOSPITALS AND HOSPICES.

AS has already been stated, from the earliest period hospitals and hospices formed an integral part of the religious establishments, such as churches, chapters, and convents of the two sexes, and of the various religious orders. For this reason, many of these at the present day are situated under the shadow of the cathedrals and churches, or, as Pastiret has expressed it, "The place of suffering and the place of prayer are both the house of God (*Maison Dieu*)."

Time, with the increase of population, and the changes in the manners and habits of the working population, particularly in large towns, have rendered these establishments unsuitable for the purpose for which they were designed. The Hotel Dieu at Paris, adjoining the church of Notre Dame, notwithstanding its many alterations and enlargements, is a striking example of this fact, and measures have been taken for its entire reconstruction. Whole blocks of houses are at the present moment (1866) being removed, greatly for the improvement of that portion of the city. Many of the hospitals are situated in ancient buildings, not originally designed for that object, giving rise to great inconvenience, and thereby inducing the administration to adopt the resolution to replace hereafter, as speedily as practicable, all such constructions by modern buildings, approved by experience and modern science. In the discussions which have arisen on the subject, some writers have expressed a regret that all hospitals are not placed outside the cities, in order to secure abundant space, light, and air, and to remove patients from the annoyances of a crowded neighborhood. Other considerations, however, have had to be weighed, and especially that of removing a patient from his family, and imposing upon friends the task of spending time and money in visiting him. Removal to a distance from home and family, and the deprivation of sympathy, would tend to exert an injurious moral effect, as the patient, in addition to disease, would be exposed to such mental distress as would act unfavorably upon his health, and diminish the chances of recovery. The first consideration in founding a hospital is the choice of a site, and this site in their opinion should be near the centre of population, so that a wounded or suffering patient need not take a long journey to enter, and so that friends could have ready access to his bedside. A space should be selected large enough to allow the buildings to be isolated from surrounding dwellings, and also to afford a garden and walks for the use of convalescents. Air and moderate exercise are important elements in the treatment of the sick, although in the English hospitals, as a rule, no suitable provision to meet this want is made, and in this respect their example is not to be followed. Tenon, many years since, in one of his treatises, says :

"The building should not be more than two stories in height, not including basement and attic. Excavate cellars, and lay lower floors three or four feet above the ground; have separated pavilions, connected by galleries. Place the least sick in the basement, those who are more sick and surgical cases in first story, and servants in basement. Isolate the wards intended for wounds and injuries, from fever and other wards."

The Hospital de Lariboisière, one of the newest establishments, has been constructed almost entirely on this plan, and is a model for other institutions of the kind. There is a deep cellar, and in the basement are kitchens, store-rooms, laundry, apothecary shop, dining-room, library, &c. The chapel is placed at the end of the court, so that patients cannot witness funeral ceremonies, while they can enter from their apartments, the men from the right side, and women from the left, and are protected from the weather when they attend daily divine service. The surgical wards are on the first story. A large space, planted with shrubs and flowers, is laid out between the pavilions, and a gallery on each side permits patients, who are too feeble to descend the stairs, to take exercise and view the garden. The buildings are situated on an elevation, and are so surrounded by wide streets as to be remote from all neighboring houses, thus presenting advantages which can rarely be obtained for such an institution in a large city.

The subject of constructing special wards for contagious diseases has lately occupied much discussion in France, and, at the request of the administration of hospitals, the Medical Faculty of Paris appointed a committee, of which Dr. Vidal was the chairman, to investigate the matter. After careful investigation a report was made, from which the following are extracts:

> 1st. Is there any necessity for separating small-pox or variolous from other patients? 2d. If so, which is the best mode of making this separation, and of preventing contagion, by placing the patient under the most favorable conditions for recovery?"

On the first question, the report endeavors to show, that all attempts made thus far to separate variolous from other patients have been ineffectual, and that under the present system the hospitals are centres for the propagation of the disease, which is spread not only through the establishments by the constant passage of patients and visitors, but through the city and its environs.

Following the example of the military hospitals, as well as those of several foreign cities, and the houses for convalescents at Vincennes and Vesinet, where distinct wards are devoted to contagious disorders, the committee recommend that the civil hospitals should follow the same plan of isolation. After having considered the second question, and after having examined the various propositions, such as the construction of separate hospitals, or a separate pavilion in each institution, or the separation of patients in different wards, they recommend the construction of a separate pavilion for the purpose in each hospital. The conclusions of the committee are summed up as follows:

"1st. It is important to separate small-pox from other patients. 2d. The good results obtained by the modes adopted at Vincennes, Vesinet, in the military and naval hospitals, and in institutions in Germany, Russia, Denmark, and Switzerland, prove the possibility of avoiding those dangers, the fear of which has prevented the adoption of these salutary measures up to the present day. 3d. The erection of a separate hospital is unnecessary, and might be attended with disadvantages. 4th. The addition to each hospital of a distinct pavilion, with a separate independent service, with wards containing from two to four beds each for small-pox and from four to six for variolous patients, with a supply of from 120 to 160 metres of air for each patient, would accomplish, as far as could be done, the separation of inmates, and would insure, as far as could be done, the conditions favorable to their recovery. 5th. In those hospitals where a separate pavilion cannot be added, it is possible as well as important to separate small-pox from other patients, by placing them in wards in a separate part of the establishment. 6th. It would be advantageous in the pavilion or hospital to reserve wards which could be occupied and vacated alternately."

The question has been much discussed as to the number of sick who can be safely admitted to any one hospital, without the risk of its becoming unhealthy in itself, or a focus of disease for the vicinity. In the opinion of the administration, a hospital should not contain more than 600 or a hospice more than 1200 beds, while other competent authority assert that, in order to secure air and insure the best sanitary conditions, the number should not exceed 300 or 400. We give below a table showing the rate of mortality of several of the principal hospitals :

	Beds.		Mortailty.
Hotel Dieu,	780		1 in 8.51
La Pitié,	580		1 " 7.81
La Charité,	484		1 " 10.0
St. Antoine,	443		1 " 8.39
Neckar,	337		1 " 7.29
Cochin,	99		1 " 7.46
Beaujou,	403		1 " 8.61
Lariboisière,	631		1 " 7.81
		Average,	1 in 8.23

It would seem that the Hospital Lariboisière, with its commanding and airy situation, its thorough ventilation, and its many appliances for the comfort and convenience of the patients, should present a better report than those less favorably situated, and yet the contrary is the fact; and the reasons for such a result seem unsatisfactory.* The differences in the mortality of the various hospitals cannot be easily explained, but depend, no doubt, in a degree, on their location, and on the nature of the diseases treated; or, as a writer has said, "Mortality does not always signify insalubrity."

Taking the facts as stated, and the light which has been elicited by the discussions of the Academy of Medicine, it

* Dr. Tardieu, one of the physicians of the hospital, among other explanations, gives the following: "This hospital is situated within the limits of the ancient suburbs of Paris, a quarter which increases rapidly from day to day. It contains a large number of manufacturing establishments, which call around them numbers of workmen, unacclimated strangers, many of them Germans, who, without direction or advice, and ignorant of our hospital arrangements, neglect the disorders to which they easily fall victims, or allow them to become serious before they apply to us for relief."

does not seem proved that the number of patients in a hospital has a decided influence on either its healthiness or mortality. These would seem to depend more upon the size and crowding of the wards, the want of ventilation, and other causes tending to the diffusion of epidemic disease. It would, then, be safe to conclude with Tenon, and other writers on the subject, that the number of patients in any one ward should not exceed 30 or 35. The wards of the Lariboisière contain 32 beds. By a regulation dated January 31, 1840, the maximum of patients in each hospital and hospice is fixed, and the beds appropriated to the various diseases, which are classed as follows: — For men — accidental injuries, fevers, scabies, syphilis, teignes. For females — injuries, fevers, scabies, syphilis, teignes, lying-in women (where no other provision is made). Also, beds for soldiers and sailors. In relation to one disease, he says:

"Many establishments do not admit cases of scabies, but it is difficult to justify such an exclusion. If we consider the rapidity with which the disorder spreads, and the ease with which modern science accomplishes its cure, we are surprised at its exclusion from most hospitals. I hereby urge you to use every means in your power to overcome this ill-founded prejudice. Such a policy would greatly benefit the poor, who are chiefly attacked, and the spread of the disease would be more easily checked by the admission of all applicants.*

* This disease is now cured in two or three hours by friction and sulphur baths. As a consequence, the wards heretofore appropriated to this class of patients are given up, and all patients treated outside the hospital. The treatment is simple, and can be used elsewhere with equal success.

"Although venereal diseases are more grave and of longer duration, and require more elaborate treatment than the one just named, the public morals and the public health require that they should not be neglected. Modern science furnishes a cure for the greater part, and alleviation for the remainder of such patients. It is important, therefore, that such sufferers should be admitted more freely than they have heretofore been. The beds apportioned to soldiers and sailors should be in proportion to the garrison, to the frequency of the passage of troops, and to the number of the maritime population. It would be superfluous to speak of the care which these men deserve, on account of their sufferings, as well as for their services to the country."

CHAPTER IX.

SITUATION AND MANAGEMENT OF HOSPITALS.

MUCH discussion has of late taken place among French physicians and surgeons in regard to the hospita plans, and particularly in connection with the re-building of the Hotel Dieu, now in course of construction at Paris. The principal points of discussion have been, first, the relative merits of hospitals established within or outside the walls of cities, and, secondly, the comparative healthiness of large and small institutions. On the first point there exists much difference of opinion. Mons. Gosselin, a professor of the school of medicine, and surgeon in La Pitié, maintains that the removal of hospitals to the country would be a great inconvenience for the sick, their families, for physicians and students, and while admitting that country air is better than city air, does not think that for that sole reason the patients would find themselves, on the whole, better off, would be more easily cured, or in greater numbers, than if they remained in Paris. On the second question there seems to be a great diversity of opinion as to the significance of the statistics furnished. Thus, Dr. Le Fort asserts that the difference in mortality between the large and small hospitals is more than one-half, while M. Gosselin asserts that the results shown by the smaller hospitals of

Paris are no more favorable than those of the larger institutions. Baron Larrey recommends very earnestly that the wards should not be overcrowded, and that patients should be scattered, and as much as possible treated at their own homes. It is well known that the latter or dispensary system has been in operation on a large scale in Paris for several years past, and that the general administration makes an annual report of its operations. From the report of 1862, it appears that the average mortality of that year, a year of usual health, in the eight general hospitals, for the medical wards, was 1 in 7.29, and for the surgical and medical departments united, 1 in 8.23. The mortality among those treated at home, and numbering 47,102, was 1 in 7.91; showing that, so far as the deaths are concerned, the plan of scattering the sick has no advantage over that of uniting them in hospitals, excepting in the case of lying-in women.

The advantages of home treatment are counterbalanced in part by the unhealthy lodgings, and the absence of the care and regimen enjoyed in the public institutions. Experience proves that the smaller hospitals have no advantage over the larger, so far as regards the rate of mortality, — the difference, as already stated, depending rather on overcrowding and imperfect ventilation. The hospitals in France do not compare in size with some of those in other countries. The hospital at Venice contains 1,200 beds; at Naples, 1,400 beds; at Berlin, 1,300 beds; at Madrid, 1,621 beds; at Vienna, 2,000 beds; at Rome, 2,000 beds; and, lastly, that of Milan is designed for 3,400 beds, and recently contained as many as

2,800 patients. The returns from these institutions do not show a greater proportion of deaths than the hospitals of Paris; and this fact, with the increased expenses necessary to carry on a larger number of smaller establishments, would seem to point out the impolicy of making any radical change in the present system.

It is not worth while here to enter upon details respecting the modes of heating and ventilating the French hospitals, as these matters can be studied with equal advantage in some of the American institutions, and particularly in the new City Hospital in Boston, which can hardly be surpassed for the perfection of its details, or in the liberality exercised by the public authorities in furnishing all the means necessary for creating a model establishment. The principal Parisian hospitals are heated and ventilated by three different plans, known as those of Duvoir, by hot water, Thomas and Laurens, by steam and hot water, and that of Hecke, by hot air alone. Thus far the preference is given by the General Director to the system last named. The engineer of the administration, Meuriene See, who was sent to England to study the comparative merits of the various systems, expresses the opinion that ventilation by mechanical means is better effected in the Beaujou, Neckar, and Lariboisière, at Paris, than in the London hospitals, where open windows and doors are depended on without reference to the inconveniences and dangers of draughts of air. Iron bedsteads have universally replaced the wooden ones formerly in use, and at the Lariboisière an elastic bed has replaced the straw mattress, which is considered objectionable. Eider down is used in some cases as an improvement on the heavy coverlets and blankets. The space between the beds varies from one to one and a half metres. The use of bed-curtains in the wards has been criticised in the discussions of the Academy of Medicine, and the example of the English hospitals in this respect extolled. It is considered generally that movable curtains, suspended loosely in large and well-ventilated wards, can produce but little injury, and that these disadvantages are more than compensated to the patients by keeping painful and disagreeable sights from their view, and by affording them a measure of seclusion. In the north of France the floors of public hospitals are washed, while in Paris, in accordance with the custom in private dwellings, they are rubbed with wax, — the physicians preferring what is called dry cleaning (*propreté seche*) to wet cleaning (*propreté humide*). In England, in many instances, patients are required to furnish and wash their own linen, while in France it is provided gratuitously. The allowance for each patient is fourteen shirts, ten pillow-cases, and sixteen sheets. For the valid and employées the allowance is eight shirts, four pillow-cases, and eight sheets; so that in furnishing a hospital of 100 beds there would be required 1,400 shirts, 1,000 pillow-cases, and other articles in proportion.

Bed and other linen, when too much worn for use, is sent to the Hospice La Salpetriere, where the old female inmates are employed for a small compensation to make it up into bandages for the use of the surgical wards in the various hospitals. The washing of the hospital linen has, until within a few years, been done by contract with parties outside the city, but many abuses having been ascertained, the administration has established laundries in the various institutions, wherever it can be done. Where there is no laundry, it is sent to some other hospital; La Salpetriere,* for instance, washing for the Hotel Dieu, the Charité, the Beaujou, and the Clinique. Contrary to the English and American plan, it is considered more cleanly and safe to furnish all patients, on entrance into the hospital, with suitable clothing, and to discard their own for the time being. From time immemorial it has been the custom in France for patients to wear a particular costume during their residence at the hospital. It is a white cotton cap, worn day and night, and until recently a long gray coat, also worn by female patients, and similar in color and shape to those worn by criminals in the prisons. With the feeling that the sick should in no way resemble the criminal, the administration, in 1858, substituted for the gray overcoat a sort of blue dressing-gown, of the same material as that worn by sailors, and being also lighter and better than the gray cloth. Ample provision is made for baths, as the use of the warm bath is much more general among all classes than in England or the United States. The most complete establishment for administering baths is connected with the Hospital St. Louis, where 108,817 were furnished to poor out-door and in-door patients in 1861. During the same year, the number of baths furnished by the various hospitals of Paris was 453,981. In 1756 there were two bath-tubs connected with the Hotel Dieu, and this was the only provision made for the sick poor of Paris.

* At the Salpetriere alone, in 1861, 3,609,368 pieces of linen were washed, at an expense of 132,399 francs.

CHAPTER X.

PRESENT SYSTEM OF PUBLIC RELIEF.

THE system of public relief of the poor, as it now exists in Paris, was organized in accordance with a law enacted in the year 1849, and is placed under the Administration Générale de l'Assistance Publique. It embraces the services of the hospitals, the hospices, and the relief of applicants at their own dwellings. The hospitals receive the sick who are susceptible of cure or relief. The hospices are intended for patients afflicted with incurable diseases, for the aged and infirm, and for children. In 1860, there were 39,000 persons in these establishments; 20,000 sick were aided at home; 60,000 were registered on the books of the Bureaux de Bienfaisance, in the different arrondissements or wards; 35,000 have been added to these numbers by the recent annexation of new quarters to the city. In 1863, the number of families relieved was 40,056, consisting of 101,370 individuals. Number of sick treated at their homes, 53,834. The director of the administration, in his report, dated June, 1864, estimates the numbers to be relieved, either permanently or temporarily, during 1865, as follows:

In Hospitals, ...	91,355
In Hospices, ...	13,134
In Convalescent Hospitals, ...	752
Abandoned children in the Foundling Hospital,	542
" " placed in the country, .	23,416
Registered poor, ...	100,000
Sick treated at their dwellings, ...	30,000
Total, ...	259,199

The whole administration of public aid (Assistance Publique) is placed under the Prefect of the Seine and the Minister of the Interior. There is a General Director, who acts under the supervision of a Board of Council. The Director is appointed by the Minister on the nomination of the Prefect. He has charge of the public hospitals, hospices, and institutions for foundlings, orphans, and insane, and prepares an annual report. The Council of Supervision consists of the Prefect of the Seine as President, the Prefect of Police, two members of the City Council, two Mayors of Arrondissements,* two Administrators of Bureaux de Bienfaisance, one Councillor of State, one Master of Requests, one member of the Court of Cassation, one hospital physician, one hospital surgeon, one Professor of the School of Medicine, one member of the Chamber of Commerce, one member of the Council of Prud'hommes, and five members taken from citizens at large. The members of the Council, with the exception of the Prefects, are appointed by the Emperor, on

* There are twenty arrondissements, with a mayor in each.

the nomination of the Minister of the Interior. Lists of candidates containing three names are enclosed to the Minister by the various bodies from which members are taken. The term of office is for two years, and members may be re-elected for a second term. The Council meets once in fifteen days, the Prefect of the Seine acting as President, and the General Secretary as Secretary of the Board. It is the duty of the Council to act upon all financial matters relating to the public establishments, upon all alterations and enlargements, as well as upon all subjects affecting their sanitary condition, and to visit them as often as may be found necessary. The hospitals are divided into two classes, general and special. The first are devoted to the treatment of acute diseases and injuries; the last to special diseases. There are eight general hospitals, viz.:

Hotel Dieu, containing 842 beds, one of the most ancient in Europe.

La Pitié, 624 beds, founded in 1612 by Mary de Medecis.

La Charité, 494 beds, founded in 1606.

St. Antoine, 352 beds, ancient abbey of St. Antoine.

Necker, 403 beds, founded by Madame Necker, in 1779.

Cochin, 125 beds, founded by Mons. Cochin, a clergyman, in 1780.

Beaujou, 440 beds, founded in 1780.

Lariboisière, founded by Madame Lariboisière, who died in 1846, leaving a bequest of 2,900,000 francs.

The special hospitals are:

St. Louis, 853 beds, founded by Henry IV. in 1607, principally for diseases of the skin, and chronic complaints.

Hôpital du Midi, 336 beds, for venereal diseases of men.

Lourcine, 276 beds, for venereal diseases of women.

Children's Hospital, founded in 1735, with a branch in the country.

St. Eugenie, 425 beds, for children.

Lying-in Hospital, 402 beds, in the ancient abbey of Port Royal.

Clinique, 146 beds, principally for lying-in patients.

Maison Imperiale de Santé, 300 beds, situated in the Rue St. Denis, and occupied by paying patients.

Beside the relief afforded by the hospitals, the general administration act as trustees of several foundations which have been established at different periods by benevolent individuals. One of the principal is that created by Mons. Anget de Monthyon, Councillor of State, who bequeathed to the hospitals the sum of 5,312,000 francs, the income of which is annually distributed by visitors at the houses of convalescents whose residence at the hospital has not been less than five days. The amount of relief given is determined by a committee, and consists of money, bread, soup, and meat. Clothing and money are given to lying-in women when they consent to nurse and take charge of their infant. The income of this fund in 1863 was 281,025 francs. There are also the —

Brezin Fund, yielding . .	189,425 francs.
Boulard " " . . .	17,809 "

Devillas Fund, yielding . .	31,177 francs.
Lambrechts " " . .	46,801 "

Under the name of hospices are included those institutions for the reception of the aged, the infirm, the insane, those afflicted with incurable diseases, destitute children, and those generally who are unable, from any cause, to obtain a livelihood. They are as follows:

Hospice for insane (men's), . .	854 beds.
Hospice " " (women's), . .	1,341 "
Hospice for old men, ...	1,705 "
Hospice for old women, . . .	2,790 "
Incurables (men), ...	427 "
Incurables (women), . . .	669 "
Ménages,* at Issy, for aged couples, widows, and widowers, . . .	1,383 "

* The Hospices des Ménages at Issy, La Rochefaucault, and St. Perine, are styled Maisons de Retraite. The first-named is new, and a magnificent institution, situated about five miles from Paris, and well worthy a visit, particularly at the season when the flowers in the courts and gardens are in bloom. Persons of both sexes are received, but applicants must either be or have been married, and have resided in the department of the Seine two years. Married couples, to gain admission, must have the united age of one hundred and thirty years, but neither must be less than sixty years old, and must have lived together at least fifteen years. Widowers and widows can be admitted after the age of sixty, but must have lived in wedlock at least ten years. The latter can occupy private rooms, or live in common dormitories, as they may elect. Applicants are admitted for life on the payment of a principal sum, or for an annual amount. For private rooms, each inmate pays on entrance 1,800 francs, or 300 francs per annum. For common room, 1,200 francs, or 250 annually. Couples occupying private rooms provide their own furniture, and clothe themselves. They receive three francs each, every ten days, a daily allowance of bread, a weekly allow-

La Rochefaucault, ... 226 beds.
Sainte Perine, ... 262 "
St. Michael, supported by Boulard Fund, 13 "
La Reconnoissance, supported by Brezin
fund, for workmen over 60 years of age, 300 "
Devillas, ... 35 "
Enfants Assistès, for foundlings, . 542 "

Besides the above there are various hospitals, civil and mili-

ance of uncooked meat, a yearly allowance of wood. Each private apartment has a small cooking-range, two closets, and box for fuel. The inmates usually cook for themselves, but those who live in the common rooms take their meals together in a common dining-room. There is a general appearance of order and neatness throughout the establishment, and the inmates, when questioned, express themselves as fortunate in having so comfortable a retreat in their old age. From the terms of admission it will be seen that this institution is not intended for the indigent, but, as expressed in the by-laws, "for those who, without being actually in a state of indigence, have not sufficient means to live." This establishment has cost about 4,500,000 francs, and is composed of several pavilions, surrounding large courts and gardens. It contains a library, reading-room, refectories, laundry, bath-house, &c. The Hospice of St. Perine was founded by M. Duckalla in 1800, and received large benefactions from the Empress Josephine. This is intended for a higher class of inmates, more particularly for old government employées who have occupied respectable positions, but have passed the period of active labor, and find themselves in reduced circumstances. There are several pavilions, surrounded by a large and beautiful park, in which the inmates take their exercise. The drawing-rooms are quite elegantly though simply furnished, and are every evening occupied by the ladies and gentlemen of the household, who amuse themselves with games and conversation. The dining-room and tables leave nothing to be desired by those who have been accustomed to the refinements of living, and the visitor can hardly fail to be impressed in this, as well as in other establishments in France, with the delicacy of feeling which prompts the authorities to make the recipients of their bounty forget their dependence in the enjoyment of such comforts, and a mode of life thus benevolently provided.

tary, not under the charge of the general administration, such as —

The new Military Hospital near Vincennes, containing	600 beds.
The Hospital of Val de Grace, with .	1,500 "
Jewish Hospital, founded by Mr. De Rothschild, ...	100 "
Asile des Vesinet, ...	300 "
Asile de Vincennes, ...	500 "

The Asile de Vesinet is situated a few miles from Paris, on the line of the St. Germain Railway, and is devoted to sick work-women. It is placed in the centre of a large park given by the Emperor. It encloses three courts, beautifully laid out, and is a model establishment in all respects, well worthy a visit. The inmates are all convalescents sent by other hospitals, and are retained three weeks in order to give them time to gain strength for a return to work. The whole establishment covers an area of one hundred acres, and has cost about 2,500,000 francs.

The asile for male convalescents is situated at Vincennes, near the walls of Paris, and covers an area of forty-two acres. The internal arrangements are similar to those of the institution at Vesinet. It contains work-shops for joiners, turners, locksmiths, tailors, and shoemakers. Workmen who have been temporarily injured in the public works are admitted free of expense. Others are admitted on payment of two francs a day, or, if unable to pay that sum, for less, on producing a certificate of indigence.

Members of mutual aid societies, and companies employing

large numbers of workmen, are admitted on the payment of a small annual subscription. If able, the workman may enter one of the shops, and be paid according to amount of work, but can leave whenever he chooses. He can also assist in keeping the grounds and garden in order, for which he receives no wages, as this is considered a recreation. As many as four hundred workmen are sometimes received during a month. The establishment keeps cows, pigs, and poultry, which are fed upon the products raised on the grounds. In passing through the various buildings, courts, and gardens of some of these establishments, the visitor might easily fancy himself in the midst of a pretty large town. The Hospice of Bicetre and La Salpetriere are of colossal proportions. The population of the latter institution at the present moment (1866) is not far from five thousand, including employées. Work-shops affording suitable employment for aged inmates have been attached to these institutions, and it is found that while affording an opportunity of gaining little sums with which to purchase luxuries that they could not otherwise enjoy, a greater benefit is obtained in the good order and cheerfulness which generally pervade the establishment. The applicant for admission must bring a certificate from the Bureau de Bienfaisance of his ward that he is in indigent circumstances, and is registered on their books. If under seventy years of age, he must produce a certificate from the physician of the Bureau that he is unable to labor; he must also bring a certificate of good behavior, and that his children and grandchildren are unable to furnish him support.

CHAPTER XI.

HOSPITAL OF LA MATERNITÉ.

AMONG the special hospitals of Paris most worthy of mention is La Maternité, occupying the ancient abbey of Port Royal, rendered famous by Pascal, and La Mère Angelique. It contains 402 beds and 80 pupils. It has two objects. It receives women in the ninth month of pregnancy, and cares for them until one week after confinement, when, if sufficiently recovered, they are discharged with their infant. The second object is to maintain a school of midwifery, to which young women from all parts of the empire can come and qualify themselves, under experienced male and female teachers, to practise the profession, with the title of "*Sages femmes.*" * Most of these pupils are sent by their department, and have to pursue a course of study lasting two years to obtain a diploma. This diploma from the Paris school gives them the first rank in the profession, and ensures them the confidence of the public. It is hardly necessary to enter into details respecting the management of this hospital, excepting so far as to give an idea of the precautions taken to obviate the dangers always attending the congregation of the class of patients for which this insti-

* The professional signs representing a mother and child are familiar to every traveller in France.

9

tution is designed. It has been proposed by some to give up the lying-in hospitals altogether, and to establish an extensive system of relief for patients at their own dwellings, as is done in London. Another plan is, to have the buildings so constructed as to have the sections independent of, and separated from, each other; so that, on the occurrence of an epidemic, the patients could be removed from one to the other, as is the case in the hospitals of Dublin and Vienna. This plan has been partially adopted in Paris, especially in the Hospital Cochin, lately rebuilt. The Minister of the Interior, in a circular dated March 25th, 1862, calls attention to certain precautions taken by Monsieur Hellot, physician of the General Hospice at Rouen, by which the mortality has been reduced one-half. The regulations are as follows:

"Lying-in patients are not admitted until the very last days of pregnancy. Patients in labor are separated from those awaiting confinement. Three distinct wards are assigned to women lately confined. These wards are large, well exposed to the sun, warmed, and carefully ventilated, containing ten beds each, though they might contain fifteen. Thirty-six metres of air are allowed for each patient. One or two of the beds are always vacant, in order to exchange whenever the condition of any patient requires it. When a ward is vacated, it is well aired during five days, at least, before occupation, and all curtains and bed-linen washed, and mattresses cleaned and renewed. New-comers are placed in the second ward, which, after being vacated, is aired and cleansed as in the first instance, and the third is then occupied. Each ward is thus, in turn, occupied and aired. To avoid the shock and anxiety which the death or severe illness of any patient might cause the others, the patient is placed in a separate chamber; or she is allowed to remain, and the others are removed. Every precaution is taken to prevent the confinement of any patient in the ward with others."

With all these precautions, epidemics occasionally prevail; and the causes and remedies are still so little understood, that the administration has not unfrequently been obliged to close the hospital.

One great object aimed at in this and similar institutions, is to induce mothers, and especially the unmarried (*filles mères*), to nurse their children. These efforts have been attended with great success; and it is found that, when once the mother has consented to nurse her infant, the natural feeling for it prevails, and she is in little danger of abandoning it, the public being thereby saved the expense of its support, or, at most, furnishing the needy mother such temporary aid as is required.

Beside La Maternité, there are in Paris several hospitals, particularly the Hospital des Cliniques, where there is a lying-in department, and a "nurses' ward," and where women who are sick, having a child less than two years of age, are admitted, or where a nursing mother is admitted with a sick child under the same age.*

* After that age, they are sent to the children's hospital.

CHAPTER XII.

INTERNAL GOVERNMENT OF HOSPITALS AND HOSPICES.

THE decree of the Minister of the Interior, of the 31st of January, 1840, is an important one, as it is that under which the hospitals of France are now administered. Its principal provisions are as follows:

"Hospitals receive sick men, women, and children, who have acute diseases, or who have been accidentally injured; also soldiers and sailors, and patients suffering from the following diseases: scabies, teigne, syphilis; also lying-in women. Some of the other diseases which may be admitted are herewith specified, besides acute diseases and wounds. I do not understand that all diseases not herein specified should be excluded, as care should be taken, in administering charitable aid, not to make the rules too arbitrary. Whenever place and circumstances permit, it would be well to admit every kind of disease. I know that the Sisters do not willingly nurse patients with every malady, as their rules prevent their caring for cases of syphilis as well as for lying-in women. These scruples should, doubtless, be respected, as everything else which relates to duty and conscience; but, nevertheless, such patients should not be neglected; and those establishments which are under the charge of Sisters of Charity will understand, that, as far as possible, these patients are to be placed in separate wards, and cared for by lay attendants.

"The hospice admits, 1st, the able-bodied aged of both sexes; 2d, incurables; 3d, orphans; 4th, abandoned children and foundlings; 5th, the aged, valid,* and incurable of both sexes, on payment of board.

"The orphans are placed under the guardianship of the various boards of administration. The sad lot of these children renders them worthy of the interest and attention of those having them in charge; but material aid is not enough. They must be taught how to provide for themselves in the future, and to become useful members of the community. They should receive in the hospice common elementary instruction, if there should be no common school in the locality which they can attend. They should be taught to labor, even when their work yields no return, in order to accustom them to habits of industry. The heavy charge devolving upon the depository hospices for foundlings and abandoned children should induce the local administrations to seek every means to lessen the evil, without neglecting the responsibilities imposed upon them by the laws in the accomplishment of their duties towards these unfortunate victims of poverty and evil passions.

"Admission to the hospitals should be prompt, as the diseases are acute, and delay might be dangerous to the patient. Except in urgent cases, admission should not be granted except by permission from competent authority, testifying to the poverty of the patient, and a certificate from a physician describing the disease. Soldiers and sailors should be received on the order of a competent authority. Lying-in women should not be admitted except in urgent cases, or until near the period of confinement, when they shall furnish a certificate of indigence. In all cases they shall be

* The French word valid, in contradistinction to invalid, is adopted as more concise and expressive than able-bodied.

discharged within fifteen days after their confinement, unless the physician shall think the discharge is attended with danger. These regulations are indispensable in order to avoid overcrowding the hospitals. In general, this latter class are admitted too early, and remain too long. A very serious inconvenience is caused by the custom of retaining children at the hospitals, when the mother has decided to abandon them. Indigence and sickness too often, unfortunately, induce the mother to neglect the duties imposed upon her by nature. For the past ten years efforts have been made, founded rather on moral than economical motives, to correct this abuse. The child is not retained unless at her formal request. When poverty and shame have tempted her to adopt this course, timely advice has often been the means of rekindling the maternal instincts, and of recalling her to a sense of duty. Many are glad to receive temporary aid for a few months, and to fulfil a mother's duties, until their health and strength allow them to gain a subsistence. The Sociétés de Charité Matèrnelle are admirable institutions for aiding poor mothers, and for inducing them to retain their children, and every effort should be made to multiply them. The Bureau de Bienfaisance will be found to be an important auxiliary. Timely aid afforded to mothers at home will prevent many from resorting to the public establishments, and thus avoid the temptation of forsaking their offspring. Physicians will report all cases which have been treated more than three months, with the reasons why they are allowed to remain. It often happens that incurables, attacked by an acute disease, are admitted to the hospitals, and after recovery remain, preventing the admission of other patients, and for this reason it is important that the physician should present this report, and enable the administration to correct abuses. When patients are pronounced incurable, they shall no longer remain in the hospital, but shall be sent to the hospice."

The Minister then goes on to urge greater care in the admission of inmates to the hospice:

"The most indigent and most infirm are to have the preference; and this is the more important as the admissions are usually for life. Applicants should be at least seventy years old, and when valid should, if possible, be assisted at home. We believe that the system of *secours à domicil* (home aid) will in the end exert a powerful influence upon the condition of the poor. In connection with institutions designed to receive those who still have a little means, it will exert a great moral and financial benefit. The committees which sustain the hospices and the Bureau de Bienfaisance will not be overburdened, for the sums given by the latter mode of relief will be more than offset by the saving made. It is merely a change in the system of relief, which will be more efficacious, and will exert a better moral effect, while it will not impose a greater burden on the public."

It is not necessary to enter into details respecting the internal management and policy of the hospitals, which differ little in this respect from well-regulated establishments in America.

In the immediate care of the sick, a great advantage is possessed in France by the devotion of women belonging to certain religious orders, or, as they are usually called, "Sisters of Charity." They have no pay, and being actuated by religious motives, they render an amount and kind of service which it would be impossible to secure from hired attendants. They are held in great esteem, and are treated with the utmost respect by physicians and patients, who usually address them as *ma mère* (my mother) or *ma sœur* (my sister). With the exception of La Maternité, Les Cliniques, L'Hospital du Midi, and the two great hospices of Bicetre and Salpetriere, these Sisters have charge of nearly every public charitable establishment in Paris. It will be remembered that some of these orders devote themselves to the sick and poor, while others are employed in instruction. The principal are the order of St. Vincent de Paul, St. Thomas de Villeneuve, St. Martha, St. Mary, and St. Augustin. The first-named order contained 5,000 members in 1846, and is now probably much more extensive. The society owes its origin to St. Vincent de Paul, who founded the system in 1633. He says of its members, "They must have no other cloister than obedience, no other grating than the fear of God, no other veil than a holy modesty." A writer says of them:

> "Under the influence of the rules adopted by the Court of Rome in 1645, this society has extended all over the world, until it has become the glory of Catholicism. It may be said, without fear of contradiction, that these holy women have gained universal veneration. They are respected in heathen lands, and in our own country, the soldier, the workman, and even religious fanaticism, has a kindly smile for the gray dress, and the broad white cap, which so often conceals a sublime self-abnegation. Voltaire, who ridiculed everything else, spared the Sister of Charity, and in our own day no sarcasms reach her."

The Sœurs Hospitalières, as they are technically called, are connected with the hospitals and hospices by a formal treaty or contract, approved by the administration and the Minister of the Interior. The Minister says in a circular:

"The care exercised by the Sisters over the hospices and hospitals is very valuable. In the greater number of these establishments they are charged under the administration with the management of the internal service. They nurse the sick, the old, the incurables, and children, with a devotion, a self-denial and patriotism, worthy of all praise. Every effort should be made to attach these pious women to the establishments, and only when they cannot be had in sufficient numbers should lay nurses be employed."

The principal conditions of the compact are as follows:

"The Sisters of the congregation of ———, to the number of ———, shall be charged with the internal service of the hospital of ———. The Superior shall render a monthly account of all moneys entrusted to her for minor expenses, but not including the sums expended for her own use and that of her companions. The number of Sisters shall not be increased without the sanction of the Minister of the Interior. In case of urgency, however, or when one of the Sisters shall be sick, so as to be unable to perform her duties, the Superior shall, at the request of the administration, procure a substitute. The Sisters shall, so far as temporal matters are concerned, be placed under the authority of the general administration. The Superior will see that good order is maintained in every department. She shall have charge of the keys, and see that the doors are closed at dark, and that they are not opened until morning, except for necessary purposes. Separate quarters near the wards shall be provided for the Sisters, and shall be properly furnished, heated, and lighted. Food and washing shall be provided them at the expense of the hospital. The administration shall allow the sum of —— francs annually for the support of each Sister, and shall allow travelling expenses. The attendants and servants shall be paid by the administration, who will appoint and discharge them at their own will, or on the request of the Superior. When age or infirmities shall render any Sister unfit for service, she may remain in the hospital, and be maintained, provided she shall have served ten years in the same, or in other kindred institution, and she shall be replaced by another. The Sisters shall, in health as well as in sickness, be considered as '*filles de la maison*' (daughters of the house), and not as mercenaries. They shall receive no boarders, nor shall they be compelled to nurse women or girls of loose morals, or patients suffering from diseases resulting from vicious courses. They shall not nurse the rich, or lying-in women, or any person outside the hospital, of any sex or condition whatever.* When a Sister dies, religious services shall be performed, and she shall be buried at the expense of the administration. In case of the withdrawal of the congregation from the hospital, the Superior shall give at least four months' notice of the intention."

The regulations in regard to these Sisters having charge of the poor, in connection with the Bureau de Bienfaisance, are very similar to those quoted above. They have distinct lodgings provided in the quarter where they are employed, often in connection with schools and work-shops for the poor of various classes. In some cases they have dispensaries con-

* This applies only to those serving in public institutions, as they are often called upon by families and strangers who are sick in Paris.

nected with the establishments, and personally prepare and administer medicines under the direction of physicians.*

Some of these establishments are very large, and include provisions for the education of the blind, the deaf and dumb, penitent girls, as well as stores and clothing for the benefit of the poor of the quarter.

* Under the ancient legislation, religious orders and communities and all others were forbidden to sell apothecaries' drugs, under a penalty of five hundred livres. A controversy having arisen, in the year ——, between the administration and the Sisters employed in the hospitals, the Minister consulted the Faculty of Medicine, and the result was the adoption of the following rules, viz.:

In hospitals confided to the care of Sisters of Charity, care should be taken to administer the medicines presented by the physicians, and to conform to all the directions given. The Sisters are allowed to prepare simple drinks, poultices, fomentations, and such simple medicines as are easily prepared, and require but little pharmaceutical knowledge. They shall not prepare officinal medicines. Officinal medicines, prescribed by the physicians, shall be delivered to the Sister by an apothecary, regularly commissioned. The Sisters shall not sell any of the medicines prepared by themselves. They shall not be allowed to prepare any kind of medicine in any hospital to which there is an apothecary attached. The latter shall be responsible for all the necessary preparations. The Minister, in a circular issued in 1838, says: "Many of the hospices and charitable institutions are conducted by Sisters of Charity, who not only prepare medicines for the sick committed to their care, but sell and distribute the same without. However praiseworthy may be the intentions of these pious women, such a practice involves certain abuses which should not be tolerated by the administration. They cannot sell and distribute remedies composed of real pharmaceutical preparations without violating the laws which regulate the profession of pharmacy, nor without exposing themselves to make mistakes of which they cannot foresee the consequences."

CHAPTER XIII.

CHILDREN'S HOSPITALS.

THE establishment of special hospitals for certain classes and diseases has been attended in France with great advantages; and this has been the case particularly with regard to hospitals for children. In former times they were placed in the same establishment with adults, where they contracted diseases more readily than others, and suffered more from the bad atmosphere around them. More than this, they were exposed to a dangerous moral atmosphere; and to obviate these dangers the administration has been compelled to provide special wards for them in those establishments where separate institutions cannot be provided, as in Paris; and experience has demonstrated the utility of the system.

A large number of the children of both sexes admitted above two years of age are affected with chronic diseases, requiring often a treatment of four, five, and six years; and during this time, it is necessary, for their future well-being, to provide them with moral and religious training, as well as the elementary branches of instruction. To meet these requirements, schools and work-shops must be furnished, with open grounds in which the little patients can enjoy the benefits of air and exercise, as well as apparatus for gymnastic exercises, now acknowledged as an important element in the treatment of many of the diseases of the young. There are two institutions in Paris thus organized; one in the Rue de Sevres, anciently called Hôpital de l'Enfant Jesus, now the Hôpital des Enfants Malades; the other in the Faubourg St. Antoine, founded under the auspices of the Empress Eugenie, and named in her honor. In connection with these, there are two establishments for scrofulous children, where the results of treatment have been much more successful than in the capital. One of these is situated in the country near Paris, at a place called Forges les Bains, the other on the northern coast at Berck, for the benefits of sea-bathing. Monsieur de Pastoret, in a report to the administration in 1816, says:

> "The establishment of a special hospital for children is a great blessing. Formerly they were placed in the same buildings with other patients, often by the side of men degraded by debauchery, and suffering from the effects of their vices. Their health sometimes suffered; their morals always. This constant intercourse with people inhabiting for a long time the same place, with the loose and familiar conversation which prevailed, produced evil effects, which often remained long after the cure of the bodily disease was effected, and left behind vicious influences which would have never existed without such demoralizing contact."

The various reasons which led to the foundation of separate hospitals for children in those days exist in still greater force to day, and their practical operation has proved their utility in Paris, as well as in other large European cities. In America separate wards have been assigned to children in various hospitals, but we believe little has been done in founding distinct establishments.

An experiment was made in 1846, by the late Amos Lawrence, of Boston, who opened a "Children's Infirmary," with thirty beds, in the southern part of the city. Several hundred patients were received during the period of its existence, which was nearly two years. The experiment was perfectly successful in its results, and was given up only on account of the large average expenditure required for so small a number of inmates. He demonstrated the fact that such an institution could be successfully established and conducted.

CHAPTER XIV.

HOSPITAL FOR CONVALESCENTS.

THESE establishments are for the benefit of patients who are sufficiently recovered to be discharged from the hospital, and, though not absolutely requiring medical treatment, are not well enough to return to their daily work. Many patients, such as journeymen, mechanics, day-laborers, and house-servants, have no home to which they can return after sickness, their places having been filled after a long absence in the hospital. The want of such an institution was felt long since in Paris, and but two institutions existed, both the fruits of private charity. One of them was attached to the Hotel Dieu, but was given up at the time of its enlargement; the second was attached to La Charité in 1656, but was given up in 1793. All were agreed as to the utility of the system as an adjunct to the hospital system, but no plan could be devised which did not involve an enormous expenditure. The present emperor, in this as well as in many other matters, was willing to *take the responsibility*, and by a decree, dated March 5, 1855, ordered the erection of two asylums or retreats, — one at Vincennes, near the walls of Paris, and the other at Vesinet, on the line of the St. Germain Railroad, a few miles distant. The latter was destined to receive male patients, convalescent from sickness, or suffering from wounds contracted in their work. By a second decree, dated August 28, 1858, it was reserved for female patients. The institution at Vincennes is for workmen, and both receive convalescents from the hospitals, as well as those who have been treated at their own dwellings, by the general administration, by the Bureau de Bienfaisance, or by the recognized mutual aid associations. These two hospitals are not subject to the general administration, but are classed with the imperial establishments *d'Utilité Publique*, and as such are under the control of the Minister of the Interior.*

These establishments are models of neatness, are placed in extensive grounds, and have every reasonable appliance for the comfort of the inmates. It is not necessary to describe the arrangement or mode of management, as they resemble other hospitals in these respects. Like every other institution, they are liable to abuses, one of which is described in a circular of the General Director as existing in these and other hospitals:

"For a long time a custom has prevailed in our hospitals which is hostile to good order, to the dignity of the administration, and a drain upon its finances. I allude to the presence of persons, who, under the name of convalescents, prolong their stay indefinitely. As assistants to the employées, officious servants of the Sisters of Charity, servants even of the house-servants, there are cases where such have remained several years at the expense of

* The other institutions of the same class are the Imperial Maison de Santé, at Charenton, the Sourds Muets, the Quinze Vingts, and the Jeunes Aveugles.

the administration, receiving at first what is allowed them in the physicians' wards, and afterwards whatever they could get by robbing other patients. They are men for the most part without a calling, morality, or means of subsistence, sometimes even fugitives from justice. Their vocation is to study the surroundings, the customs, and characters, and to win the good-will of the Sisters, to insinuate themselves into the good graces of patients, and to obtain what they can by importunity or by fraud. Obsequious and attentive to those who have means, they watch their last hours, in order to rob them of whatever little articles they may have placed under their dying pillow. This kind of hanger-on, so annoying and dangerous, ought to disappear from our establishments, and the administration can no longer tolerate them without incurring just blame, without violation of good faith, or without failing in its duty towards the sick intrusted to its care."

The circular concludes by calling upon Directors, physicians, and Sisters of Charity, to ferret out and expel the guilty parties.

Two retreats for the convalescent children from the hospitals of Paris have been recently founded: one, devoted to boys, at La Roche Guyon, by the Count de la Rochefaucault; the other, for girls, at Epinay, by the physicians of the hospitals of St. Eugenie and of the Enfants Maladès. Both are placed under the patronage of the Emperor, whose physician, Mons. Conneau, is the Director of the last named institution.

CHAPTER XV.

USE AND ABUSE OF HOSPITALS.

AS has been already stated, the hospitals and hospices have a common origin, and differ but little in their external organization. They are supported by the same revenues, and are governed by the same administration. They differ principally in the nature of the diseases and sufferings which they are destined to alleviate.

However alike the organization of the two, the requirements are very different in all that pertains to the internal regulations and management. Thus the patient who enters the hospital temporarily finds himself in a very different position from that of the old man or cripple who enters the hospice for life. The obligation to labor when possible, imposed upon the latter, cannot of course be applied to the former. The latter class must also necessarily be subjected to more stringent police regulations, in order to control the large number of aged and infirm, many of whom have contracted vicious habits which it is found difficult to overcome. They are admitted gratuitously, and are all absolute paupers. There is another class of institution much preferable to the common hospices, because it has none of the elements of a pauper institution, or anything which can lessen the self-respect of its beneficiaries, but, on the contrary, enables them to look upon the relief obtained as the result of their own foresight and industry. This is a special institution, or a ward set apart in some existing hospice, where the aged are received, and provided for during life, on the payment of a fixed principal sum, or at an established rate of board, the city or the department being the guarantee of the fulfilment of the conditions, and thus securing a certainty for the future which no private charitable organization could furnish. The prospect of such a retreat in case of need, after the labors of life are past, is found to act as an incentive to economy, and, consequently, to other virtues. The benefits arising from this system are now so fully appreciated that every facility is given for its extension throughout France.

It is evident that such an institution has every advantage over the common hospice. It tends to the same general result as the Savings Bank and Caisse de Retraite, hereafter mentioned. It promotes habits of thrift and good order, in giving the workmen a fixed object and an inducement to the practice of economy and thrift. The same principle applies to other classes, for whose benefit similar institutions are open, according to their means and requirements.

Great care is exercised in the admission of applicants to the common public hospices, as they offer inducements to the poor to stifle the natural instincts, and to forget the most sacred obligations. The aged, as soon as they can no longer contribute to the common stock, or have become burdensome to the children, are thrown upon the charity of the public. The opinion is too often held among the poor that the hospice is created for their convenience, to aid them in relieving themselves of their relatives, when they have become incapacitated for labor by age or infirmity. In Paris no applicant is admitted until his case has been investigated by a visitor, and reported upon by a committee of the general administration. In the departments the case is brought directly before the administration. The condition of the candidate, with that of his family, his moral character, and the question whether his children or relatives can support him, are investigated. In a circular, dated January 31st, 1840, the Minister of the Interior says:

"We are not speaking of patients who are attacked by acute and temporary sickness, who must be relieved without delay, as a measure of policy as well as of humanity, but of persons more or less in need, whom we must receive for a lifetime, and who become a public charge for an indefinite period. If age alone is considered as a qualification for admission, the candidates must be so numerous that all cannot be received. In view of this fact, the administration should carefully weigh the duty imposed upon it in the premises, and since a choice must be made among the number, is it not more natural and more charitable to refuse admission to the able-bodied, until those more to be pitied have been provided for? The aged who are able-bodied have less need of public aid than the others, for old age is often vigorous among the laboring classes, and does not interfere with certain kinds of light work, by means of which an appeal to public charity might be avoided. This class then should be received only with rare exceptions into the hospices, and I do not hesitate to say that the too great facility for the admission of such cases is one of the most common causes of embarrassment to the administration. It is not only in a financial point of view that I call your attention to the subject; a question of public morality is involved. The truth of this assertion is shown by the desire, and even persistence, with which children seek to place parents in the hospices. While in some places great repugnance is shown to entering the hospitals, there exists among the poor an earnest desire to enter the hospice themselves, or to place their parents there. In the first instance, it is to leave a mother or a child for a few days; while in the seeond it is a separation for life. The cause of this humiliating fact is found in the often-expressed idea that the family should be relieved from the burden of maintaining those who can earn nothing for the common support. With the aid of the hospice for the aged and for children, the anti-social and inhuman idea is too often entertained that we owe nothing to those beings who are useless to us, and while some are ashamed to ask admission to a hospital for themselves, they are willing to rid themselves forever of those who should be most dear to them. Experience shows that a too ready charity, extended to certain classes of the poor, destroys the finer sentiments which should prevail in the family circle. This result has too often been observed in regard to the hospices for the aged, and should excite the attention of the administration."

The Minister further expresses the opinion that incurables should be classed with the sick, and for that reason they deserve more consideration than those who are able-bodied, and who, as he considers, are unjustly preferred in many public institutions. The able-bodied are by law excluded from the hospice until they are seventy years old, and those who have not reached that age are within the province of the Bureau de Bienfaisance. In Paris two years' residence is required, and in the departments usually a longer time, in order to gain admission. The subject is not regulated by law, but is left to the various local administrations. Labor in the hospices is compulsory, and whoever refuses is liable to punishment. The penalties are confinement, public reprimand, and loss of privilege to leave the premises.

The Director is bound to furnish employment, suited to the strength and capacity of the inmates. Two-thirds of the product of labor is paid into the treasury, and the remaining third is given to the inmates, once in ten days, or at such time as may be thought best in each case. In order that the kinds of employment shall not interfere with other branches of industry, it is recommended that only such articles be manufactured as shall be required for furniture or use by the various charitable institutions under the government of the administration. Experience has shown that a form of light labor suited to each inmate has the effect of giving him wholesome exercise, thereby lessening the tendency to infirmities, and prolonging life, while entire idleness has a directly contrary effect. With idleness the strength soon fails, *ennui* supervenes, and those inmates who have hitherto led a laborious life find that the coveted inactivity is only a means of decay and death. Beside the hygienic advantages, it is found that the system of employment tends greatly to promote cheerfulness and good order, while the little sums gained act as a stimulus, in enabling them to procure little luxuries of which they would otherwise be deprived.

CHAPTER XVI.

RETREATS.

WHEN once the applicant to the hospice or almshouse is successful in gaining admission, he becomes an acknowledged pauper, considers himself no longer obliged to make further exertion, and has only to enjoy the repose which he thinks himself entitled to, after his long years of labor and perhaps improvidence. There is in Paris another class of institution, already alluded to, which has many advantages, in that it allows the inmates to maintain their self-respect, and to enjoy a rest without the sense of obligation to the public.

These establishments are called "Hospice à prix de Pension," or retreats, and are adapted to various classes, though differing in extent and resources. The Maison de Retraite de Rochefaucault, for instance, admits applicants not less than sixty years old, on the payment of a sum graduated according to age, or for an annual sum of 250 francs for those in health, and 312 francs for those who are disabled and infirm. There is also the Hospice des Ménages, a new and splendid institution, lately removed from the interior of Paris to Issy, a village in the suburbs. This is devoted to aged couples, widowers and widows, who have resided ten years in the Department of the Seine. The arrangements are so made as to accommodate these three classes in separate chambers, or in large common dormitories, as may be preferred, or according to the means of the inmates. The married couples enjoy for life a good chamber of moderate dimensions, with closets and cooking apparatus, and various conveniences, on the payment of a capital sum of 3,200 francs. Widowers and widows have a smaller chamber, and pay 1,600 francs, while those who live in the dormitories pay 1,000 francs. There are extensive grounds attached to the establishment, with library and drawing-rooms, where the inmates assemble in the evening for conversation and games. On birth and *fête* days the chambers of the old couples often become a rendezvous for whole families of different generations, where kindly feelings and greetings are interchanged. This hospice is new, a model of its kind, and is one of the most interesting charities in France. The best proof of the popularity of the system is, that, in the various establishments, there are many more applicants than can be admitted, and applicants are sometimes obliged to wait their turn of admission for years. In the mean time the little capital is wasted, and instances have been known where the means have been exhausted while waiting admission, and the applicant has been thrown upon the public for support. On this subject the Minister of the Interior thus expresses himself, in a circular dated Jan. 31, 1840:

"If there be any mode of exercising charity, at once useful to the recipient and creditable to those who bestow it, it is certainly in receiving aged people into comfortable homes, on terms founded on the probable cost of their support. These terms should be so moderate that persons with the smallest incomes could afford to enter, without, however, imposing loss upon the hospice. The economy secured by providing for a large number should attain this end. Thus the evil results which I regretted in speaking of the free admission of the aged to the public hospices would not be seen. The idea of retiring in old age to a respectable retreat, not at the charge of the public, because he pays for his own support, should be agreeable to an honorable man, and should promote the practice of such economy as would enable him to be independent during his later years. There are not many such establishments in France. Paris possesses only a few, and it often happens that years pass before an applicant can obtain admission. It is therefore in this direction that charitable efforts should tend. In towns where there are no buildings suitable for a separate institution, proper apartments could be reserved. They could be increased as wanted, devoted to the different classes, and the regimen made to correspond to the sum paid, always differing from that of the free inmates. It is easy to imagine the good results to which these institutions would lead. If well administered, much good might be done without taking anything from the amount usually bestowed in private charity, and without burdening the community with increased expenditures. I will add that after the hospices or the towns shall have incurred the first outlay for establishing and even supporting these institutions, they will be compensated for their expenditure by the smaller number of poor requiring gratuitous support."

A plan has been followed in some countries, particularly in Switzerland, of placing the aged poor on farms, at a fixed rate of board, and of making them as useful as their age and strength would permit, by furnishing them with suitable employment. This custom has not prevailed in Paris, excepting in regard to infirm and idiotic children. It is urged that, for the old as well as for the adult, reared in the city, and with habits formed, such a change in the mode of life would not be free from danger; and that to deprive them of the consolations of occasional intercourse with family and friends would tend to foster *ennui*, expose them to home-sickness, or sever those domestic ties which a residence at the hospice might weaken but not destroy.

HOSPICE DE SAINTE PERINE.

This establishment is conducted on the same principles as the two last named, and was formerly situated at Chaillot, near Paris. It was founded during the last century by Monsieur Chausseret, and after his death fell into the hands of speculators, from whom it was rescued by the Empress Josephine, whose name is now attached to one of the principal pavilions. By a decree dated May 10th, 1807, it was placed under the General Administration de Bienfaisance Publique, and has since been transferred and rebuilt on a magnificent scale at the village of Anteuil. It consists of several distinct pavilions, entirely isolated the one from the other, each devoted to a particular class of inmates, viz., married couples, widowers, and widows, and contains in all two hundred and sixty-eight chambers. The design of this institution is to furnish a respectable retreat in old age for government employées, their families, and other persons who have occupied respectable positions in society, but have been reduced in their circumstances.

In a report of a special commission appointed to reorganize the establishment, Monsieur Ferdinand Barrot, the chairman, says:

"Your sympathy is not asked for an ordinary class of the poor; there is another kind of poverty, brought about by some sudden reverse in fortune, which overtakes a family hitherto prosperous. Sometimes it is the artist, whose hand is paralyzed, or whose eye-sight has failed, and who falls in the contest which he has carried on for the sake of fame rather than fortune. Sometimes it is a poverty entailed by the death of an illustrious man, or a widow, or cherished daughter. This kind of poverty is attended with cruel suffering. It is surprised at itself. Its own souvenirs are the poisoned arrows which wound. In looking upon the past, it sees only happy and prosperous days. It turns away with a kind of terror from the idea of a hospice, to which it has not been accustomed. We ask you to make St. Perine a home where misfortune shall find aid and commiseration, and where a hand shall be extended not only to relieve, but to encourage."

Applicants are received after the age of 60 on the payment of 700 francs per annum, or on the payment of a capital sum graduated according to age. The capital sum required is 6,348 francs at the age of 60, and 900 francs at 95 and above. The guarantee for a permanent support is furnished by the city of Paris, through the General Administration, and thus it possesses a great advantage over any private association in the confidence inspired as to its permanence and stability. Application for admission is made at the central office of the administration, and a certificate must be produced, showing whether such applicant is married or single, whether he has children, the position he has occupied, present means of subsistence, age, and whether he has lived ten consecutive years in the Department.

The administration is bound to investigate the moral character and the responsibility of those who are named as sureties for the payment of dues. Attention is paid also to the physical condition of the applicant. Admission is granted by the General Director in the order of application, preference being given to those who have reached the age of eighty. The inmates, on entrance, furnish their own rooms, are lodged, fed, and have their washing done. They are cared for when sick, have the benefit of the extensive grounds and gardens, and the use of the library and drawing-rooms, which are well warmed and lighted. Meals are served in the general dining-room, which, in its furniture and equipment, resembles the same apartment in a first-class hotel. In case of sickness, or when the inmate is too aged or infirm to go to the common table, meals are furnished in the private rooms. The boarders have the care of their own rooms, and provide their own clothing, fuel, and lights. The furniture of the apartments is kept in repair by the administration, and remains with them on the death of the inmates. In case of serious disorder, or infraction of the rules, the offender may be discharged from the institution, and no one is allowed to remain who shall, after his entrance, receive from any source sufficient means for his support outside the hospice. No pension beyond the sum of 640 francs per annum shall be allowed to any pensioner who, after having paid in a capital sum, shall, for any reason, leave the hospice.

The annual sum required formerly for admission to St. Perine was 600 francs, but has recently been raised to 700, a price which, at the present advanced cost of all the necessaries of life, does not nearly meet the expenses. The annual cost of each inmate to the institution, by last report, is 1,260.74 francs.

Monsieur Chardon Lagache, a merchant of Paris, has recently founded a large establishment, conducted on the same principle as the others. It is situated at Anteuil, and, we believe, is placed under the control of the General Administration, Monsieur C. paying a large annual subscription towards its support.

CHAPTER XVII.

SECOURS À DOMICIL, OR HOME-AID FOR THE SICK.

FOR convenience, as the French title is a long one, we will call this the system of home-aid, which was regularly organized in Paris in the year 1853, though previously tried in the sixth arrondissement by Mr. Vee, the mayor, and formerly a Director of the General Administration de Bienfaisance Publique. No better idea can be formed of the plan than is furnished by the following quotations, taken from the Code des Hôpitaux:

"The system of home-aid is perhaps the most interesting branch among the public charities, of which the public hospitals and hospices should be only the supplement. The last are essential to persons who find themselves in a state of complete destitution, without relations, friends, or means of subsistence; but with the convenience of the system of home-aid, the number of those seeking admission may be diminished by helping them to remain with their families. It is more gratifying to the sick or disabled man to be aided at his own dwelling, and to enjoy the care of his family and friends, than to find himself isolated in a hospital, and surrounded only by persons with whom he has no ties of blood or friendship. The community cannot fail to gain by this kind of relief, which tends to strengthen the family ties, and to encourage parents and children to fulfill the duties imposed upon them by nature."

In France, as elsewhere, the country people have a strong antipathy to the hospital, and only resort to it in the last extremity. The prejudice is shared more or less in the capital, and is not entirely without foundation, although the poor patients enjoy there a care which they cannot have at their homes, and which the Sisters of Charity know so well how to bestow. They are also treated by physicians enjoying the greatest public confidence; still they suffer more or less from the depression arising from the separation from friends, uneasiness on account of their families, the sight of fellow-sufferers, and, not the least, from the loss of personal identity, which they leave at the hospital gate, and are only known by the number of the bed they occupy.*

However great the objection to the hospital, made by some, it is a most convenient resource for the unmarried, the

* Extract from an address delivered by the Director of the Administration Generale at the distribution of prizes to the hospital medical pupils, Dec. 26, 1854:

"Your instruction and the claims which science has upon you are but secondary to those of your unfortunate clients. Here, gentlemen, and I speak to all, the poor who suffer have a right to all the kindness and attention you can afford, consistent with the obligations which your duties impose upon you. There are susceptibilities in our fellows which it is due to ourselves to respect. What is more painful, I might say humiliating, to the unfortunate patient admitted to your hospitals, than to be obliged to sacrifice his individuality, to renounce, as it were, the man, to become an abstraction, a number, — the thing in fact which you call, in the language of the schools, a *subject*. Beware, I beseech you, lest, in the preoccupation attendant upon your studies, the man entirely disappear from your view, and the subject remain. Need I remind you of the agony, the moral torture, inflicted upon those unfortunate women and poor young girls, so much to be pitied, by those daily, almost public examinations, required, I know, for your instruction, and yet hateful, unless accompanied by all the consideration compatible with inexorable necessity. What disgust, what repugnance, should not be felt, in such exigencies, by virtuous minds, and how great should be your care to soothe the poor sufferers, and to help them to undergo the trial."

person without a home, or for the stranger who is attacked by illness. For many of the poor also, who have dark and badly-ventilated dwellings, and who cannot obtain the comforts of life, or for those who are to undergo severe operations, the hospital offers a desirable refuge. The poor in France have, for a long period, been classed as the able-bodied without work, the sick, and the disabled or infirm. The object has been to find work for the first-named, while the others were sent to the hospitals, hospices, and Maisons Dieu, and those having a lodging were relieved at home. By an edict of Henry II., in the sixteenth century, it is declared:

> "The king wills that all the sick and infirm poor who have houses, chambers, or lodgings, in the city or suburbs of Paris, shall be fed, assisted, and cared for, by the parishioners of the respective parishes in which they are found; and to this end they shall cause the curate, vicar, or marguillier, to make a record of all such, each in his church or parish, and to give aid at their homes, or at such other place as they may think proper. Neither they nor their children shall beg or ask alms, under penalty of a whip for adults, and a rod for the children; and for this object shall be appropriated such moneys as shall be collected in churches or private houses in said parishes."

This system of compulsory aid resembled somewhat the English poor-tax, though the legal right to a support was never established in France. In 1544, Francis I. established a Board of Overseers of the Poor, consisting of thirteen citizens and four counsellors, who were authorized to levy a poor-tax on all princes, seigneurs, clergy, communities, and private estates. The lists of the poor were drawn up by special committees, who were charged with the duty of distribution. In the provinces the same duties were entrusted to the curates and marguillers, assisted by lady visitors. The system underwent various changes until the revolution of 1792, when nearly every charitable institution was swept away, and a law was passed requiring each department to take care of its own poor. After the confiscation of the hospitals and other charitable institutions, the government failed to fulfil its pledges for the support of the poor, more as a matter of necessity, caused by the general financial distress, than from any deliberate violation of faith. In 1793 an attempt to reorganize the charitable establishments was made without success. The only provisions of this project worth recording were those which served as a basis for legislation at a future date, and were as follows, viz.: To provide work for the able-bodied poor; home-aid for the disabled and their children; aid for the old and the sick who had no domicil; admission to the hospices for abandoned children, the aged and disabled without domicil, and aid for the wounded; the establishment of a National Provident Institution for those citizens who wished to make a provision against future need, thus initiating in France the system of savings banks.*

A law, passed on the 22d Floreal, year 2, decreed the formation in each department of a national charitable list, on

* The first savings bank in Paris was founded in 1818, by an association of bankers and capitalists, under the presidency of James Lafitte, governor of the Bank of France; other cities soon followed the example, and the whole system is now regulated by the act of June 30, 1851.

which should be inscribed the names of certain classes, who should have a right to public annual aid to the amount awarded to their class.

From a report made 1854, it appears that in 1847 there were 31,820 communes or villages in France, out of which only 9,336 had a Bureau de Bienfaisance. The whole population at that time was 35,400,486. The 9,336 possessing bureaux contained a population of 16,521,883, thus leaving the poor among more than one-half the population to depend on voluntary charity. The expenses for the bureaux during the year were 16,885,215 francs, and an average of 12.90 centimes for each poor person. Deducting expenses of administration, the actual average sum received by each was 10.42 centimes. Some of these bureaux were of very little importance, as 145 of them reported an annual income of less than 10 francs; 226 possessed from 10 to 20 francs; 258 from 20 to 30 francs; and the receipts of 17 of them varied from 51 centimes to 9.25 centimes. During the prevalence of the cholera in 1849, the experiment was made of furnishing the sick poor what was called secours d'hospice (hospital aid), which is the more worthy of record, as it has been continued since that time with good results. The number of deaths being very large in the two great establishments of Bicetre and La Salpetriere, the administration took advantage of the circumstance to inaugurate this system of charity. In the first-named hospice, 300 beds, and 500 in the latter, were removed, and the estimated cost for maintaining each was appropriated for the relief of some patient at his own dwelling. The sum fixed upon was 253 francs for men, and 195 francs for women. In 1860, on account of the annexation of suburbs to Paris, the number of patients thus treated was increased to 1,137.*

Among other charitable associations in Paris for the relief of the poor at their homes, is the Société Philanthropique, founded in 1781, of which the Duke de Rochefaucault Liancourt is chairman. Six dispensaries are established in different quarters of the city, where medical advice and medicines are gratuitously afforded. Physicians also visit patients who cannot leave their dwellings. The society possesses ten ovens, from which they distribute, by tickets, portions of rice, beans, soup, and boiled beef. In 1862, 290,016 portions were distributed Similar associations exist in some of the large manufacturing towns for the benefit of workmen and their families.

* In order to receive this allowance, the patient must be at least 70 years old, must have a furnished room or lodging, and should have been on the poor-list for at least one year. From November to April, the sum allowed to men is 24 francs per month; for women, 18 francs. During the other seven months, 19 francs for men, and 15 francs for women.

CHAPTER XVIII.

HOUSES OF REFUGE.

THIS title is given to establishments formed for the reception of various classes, but all having the same general object. One is intended for able-bodied laborers who may be thrown out of employment, and are expected to work, while they remain, at less than the common standard of wages. Another is destined for the reception of discharged convicts, who, on account of their precedents and character, are unable to find employment on their leaving prison. A third is for the benefit of servants while seeking place. Another is for the reception and moral improvement of girls of loose morals seeking reform. Most of these institutions are conducted by Sisters of Charity, and answer an excellent purpose. The principal objection made to them is of an economical kind, though their moral benefits are generally acknowledged. They offer a degree of competition by cheap labor to industrial establishments engaged in the production of the same fabrics, thus tending to a reduction of price, diminution of wages, and to the aggravation of the evil which they are designed to remedy. It is sometimes impossible to dispose of the products of the work-shops, and this obliges the administration to curtail the admissions, at the very time when financial embarrassments or depression in business make the refuges most necessary. If the products are suddenly thrown upon the market, a forced sale at low prices acts injuriously upon manufacturers producing similar articles, and consequently upon the interests of the workmen employed. It is found necessary to exercise great care in this matter, and some of the large towns employ their poor almost wholly in agricultural labors, in order to avoid these objections. No refuge can be established, unless temporarily, without permission of the government. They are supported by private subscriptions, by the sale of the articles produced, and by grants from the towns where they are situated. Any inmate can send a petition to the public authorities without submitting it to the director. The authorities committing any inmate have always the right to enter the refuge and communicate with him. There is in Paris an institution of this kind, called the Refuge de St. Michel, which is conducted by Sisters of the religious order bearing that name.

CHAPTER XIX.

THE CRÈCHE.

THE crèche is an establishment for the reception of infants, where they are cared for during the day, while their parents are employed at their work.

The first crèche in France was founded about fifty years ago by the Marchioness de Pastoret. The history of that event is related as follows:

"One day, as Madame de Pastoret was climbing a narrow stair to administer aid to a poor woman who lived in the fifth story, she was startled by distressing cries from a neighboring room. The cries were those of a child, who seemed to have no one near to pacify her. On knocking at the door, there was no answer. On knocking still louder, she could get no reply; she could only hear the smothered sobs of the little child. Disappointed, she ascended to the room of the poor woman whom she had come to visit, and for the first time, forgetting the suffering before her, she made inquiries respecting the neighbors. 'You need not be surprised,' answered the woman; 'it is the common fate of all of us who become mothers. What can we do? Can we leave our work? Who then would care for our families? Can we work at home? Who then will give us anything to do? Have we accommodations in which we can carry on our trade at home? Can we work enough to obtain a living, burdened as we are with the care of our children, and even impeded in ourlabors by their caresses?' 'You are, then, in the habit,' replied Madame de Pastoret, with emotion, 'of leaving your children alone during the whole day?' 'Oh, not exactly,' replied the woman. 'Sometimes we leave them with a neighbor, or with some older child. But sometimes our neighbor is sick, — just my case at present, — and sometimes the older children are the cause of accident rather than a protection, on account of their turbulence or ill-temper.' Madame de Pastoret could hear no more, and after giving to her poor patient what she had brought her, she hastily left, impressed with the new kind of suffering thus for the first time revealed to her. She proceeded at once to the shop of a locksmith, and immediately brought him back with the request that he would force the lock of the chamber from whence the cries had issued. On entering she found a little girl, who had retreated with a frightened look to the corner of the room, while a little child, two years old, struggled convulsively upon the floor at her feet. To reassure the eldest child, and to draw from her a confession of what had happened, and which was too plainly evident, was the work of a few moments. She had permitted the little one confided to her charge to climb upon a bureau, and the child had fallen upon the floor and broken its arm. They were shut in, and unable to get assistance, as the mother had calculated only upon the dangers of the stair-way and the street. Frightened at the fall of the little sister, without comprehending the gravity of the accident, the elder child had hidden herself in the corner, and there remained silent during Madame de Pastoret's first attempts to enter. Fortunate hazard! or rather, admirable Providence, who had allowed this incident to cross the path of one so disposed to improve it."

A house was soon hired near the church of St. Phillipe du Roule and the corner of the Rue Verte, and twelve poor children were received and placed under the care of a Sister of Charity, named Sister Françoise, who continued to manage the institution during thirty years, and, by her zeal and intelligence, contributed much to its success, and thus furnished a model which, at a later period, led to the foundation of similar establishments in Paris and other parts of France. The work was further continued and improved at a later period by Mons. Marbeaux, who entered warmly into the plan, and was the means of its still more general adoption.

Nothing would seem more worthy of patronage than the plan of gathering in the children of the poor, and thus presenting them to the care and sympathy of ladies of the wealthier classes, who are enabled to exercise their charitable feelings in a most useful and attractive manner. Everything, at first sight, would seem to favor such an institution. To offer to the poor laboring woman a home for her child while she is engaged about her daily labor, with the privilege of returning and nursing it during the day, would seem to be a boon which no one could gainsay. Notwithstanding such apparent advantages, some doubt the soundness of the reasons which led to the establishment of the "crèche." The General Administration of Assistance Publique has thus far refused to incorporate the crèche into the system of public charity. A report of that body, made in 1849, contains the following:

"To keep the precious and feeble being to which she has given birth, to fold it to her bosom and nourish it, such is the important duty which God and nature have imposed upon the mother, — a duty which she is happy to fulfil when no unfavorable circumstances intervene to prevent it. And this is the case when the father, understanding his obligations, provides by his labor for all the wants of his wife and his children. Nevertheless, our social duties, and the numerous wants to which they give rise, often disturb this harmony. In the household of the poor, the woman must necessarily work hard. The gains of the two hardly suffice for subsistence, and the birth of the infant increases the expenses by new wants, and imposes new labors on the poor mother. Thus fresh struggles are required and new expedients are necessary. Often an aged mother or aunt, herself past the season of labor, undertakes in part the care of the child, in order that the daughter may have the benefit of her own labors. A fortunate and desirable state of things, a happy and holy association, which binds together the three generations by the most elevated considerations of duty and gratitude. Sometimes, and still happier for all, there are in the household other children, the eldest of whom can take charge of the new-comer. Their intelligence is quickened, and if you observe the family, you will discover with pleasure, in such children, the gradual growth of the purest and best interests of humanity. Unfortunately, every family does not consist of such happy elements. Often the young mother is obliged to entrust her infant to mercenary hands, and often she does not even possess the small means to enable her to do this. Her resources fail, and her poor dwelling becomes the scene of sadness and despair.

"The present charity comes, then, in good time for her relief. It says, Go wherever your duty may call you, and in the mean time we will give a cheerful and safe asylum to your child, where it shall receive all needful care; you shall nurse it, if you will, during the day, and when the day is past, you shall carry it home, where its smile shall reward you for the labor which ensures your existence as well as its own. Each day you can do the same thing, and with the same feeling of security. The voice which speaks thus is that of the founder of the crèche, and the language shows sufficiently the benefits of the system. These benefits have conditions which must not be lost sight of when we are called upon to supply the means from the resources of private, and especially of public, charity. These conditions require that the crèche should be within a limited space and within a convenient distance of the mother's dwelling; that too large a number should not be gathered in one place, where they would be exposed to epidemic diseases peculiar to that age; that they should be placed in the localities where most needed, and this, it cannot be disguised, will augment the expense."

The report expresses a fear that the crèche may have an injurious effect upon the family relations of the poor, and goes on to say:

"If the mother is taken away from the calling which enabled her to meet the expenses of the household, increase the amount of her allowance, to recompense her for her forced idleness, but take good care not to disgust her with the duties of home, her true field, or to lead her to consider her fecundity as a misfortune, or to lessen the attachment which all beings naturally feel for their offspring. If the crèche can be extended, and become one of our institutions, without weakening the feelings of maternity, without lessening family ties, without lessening the tenderness brought out in the education of the infant; if there be no danger to society that children, given up to strangers, become hereafter a generation without ties or restraint, whose existence too often begins in vice and ends in crime, then let us leave to private charity the task of making the experiment and of demonstrating its success."

In commenting on the above, a writer says:

"This argument is unjust, so far as it exaggerates the evils of a principle laid down too strongly. In the first place, the crèches are allowed only as a means of relief for poor mothers, under certain circumstances, and intended for those only who can do no better. In allowing the mother to nurse her infant during the day, and retaining it during the hours of labor, the crèche offers no more objection in principle than giving it up to the care of a stranger, in placing it with a nurse, or other of the usual methods."

M. Dupin, president of the Société des Crèches, at its meeting in 1847, expresses himself thus:

"The crèche is not only a help to the infant: it aids also the virtuous mother and the family of the honest poor. We do not take the child from the mother; we merely borrow it in order to aid her, to supply her place, and to encourage her while engaged in the necessary duties for gaining her livelihood."

However little ground there may be to objections, there are certain inconveniences in the practical operation of the system which cannot be overlooked. The greatest objection is the assembling under one roof too large a number of little children, no matter how cleanly and well-aired the place, or how good the management. Experience has shown that there is much danger from the prevalence of eruptive fevers, ophthalmias, and other diseases. From an investigation, made by the general administration in 1853, it was shown that, of 512 infants placed in the fourteen crèches of Paris, 222, or more than two-fifths of the number, died, whereas the rate of mortality among children in the capital, from one day to three years of age, was only one in four. Another cause of this mortality is the exposure of the children in all weathers in their passage to and from the crèche. It cannot be expected that the young child, who has passed the day in a warm and well-ventilated apartment, and been supplied with all the comforts which an active charity can administer, can safely return to the cold and dreary lodging of its parents, deprived, as it usually is, of common comforts. Another cause of mortality is the long-continued recumbent position of the children during the day, for lack of a sufficient number of nurses and attendants.

CHAPTER XX.

CRÈCHES.

THE crèches, which were originally established in Paris, for children under two years of age, where mothers had to seek work outside their own dwellings, are now very generally occupied by children who have been weaned, or who have passed the prescribed age. According to the last report of the inspector, of the 544 children in the crèches of Paris, only 188 were nursed by their mothers. It is a significant fact that the working population of Paris, as well as of the departments, seem little anxious to avail themselves of the benefits of the institution. In 1849 it was found that only one crèche in fourteen was filled; of the 398 beds contained in all the crèches of Paris, but 274 were occupied. In 1853 there were twenty-five crèches, of which only three were filled. Of the 780 beds, 544 were occupied and 236 were vacant, the proportion being nearly the same as in 1849. It has been found that the mothers who availed themselves of the institution did not continue to do so for a long time. The average stay of each child is sixty-two days, thus making an almost entire change of inmates every two months. The economical aspect of the question is of importance. The average cost of each child is sixty-two centimes per day. A good nurse can be procured for sixteen or eighteen francs per month, which would make the cost fifty or sixty centimes per day. As an economical question merely, it would seem that the advantages are on the side of the plan of hiring nurses. These facts would seem to give weight to the opinions expressed in the report of a commission at a session held in Paris, May 26, 1853:

"The crèches have been diverted, and happily so, from their original purpose. Established originally for children under two years of age, and especially for nursing children, to allow their mothers to attend to their daily work, they are now occupied by weaned children, and this class is constantly increasing. We are persuaded that, so far as the nursing children are concerned, it would be better to loan a cradle to the mothers, to furnish clothing and a portion of the cost of retaining the child at the crèche, and when the mother has to seek employment elsewhere than at home, a portion of the money could be given to some poor neighbor, who would take charge of a few small children during the day, and thus serve a double purpose. The children of those who could not nurse them could be placed in charge of country nurses without increased cost."

The advocates of the institution insist that, although the system may not be applicable to Paris, it would be entirely so in the centres of population in the great manufacturing cities, where the majority are workmen, and where the residences of this class are near their place of employment, and mothers could easily avail themselves of the privilege. By an act dated Feb. 26th, 1862, the crèches and some other kindred institutions are placed under the patronage and protection of the Empress. All these, as well as others sustained by private liberality, are subjected to certain rules, principally of a sanitary character. Notwithstanding the encouragement afforded by the government, and the safeguards placed around these establishments, they do not seem to be universally appreciated. A circular issued Nov. 28th, 1862, says "the statistics which have been furnished show that while the crèches prosper in some departments, they work poorly and are little appreciated in others," and urges the Prefects to make the advantages of the system better known, in order that it may be more generally adopted by the local authorities. In a meeting of the association held in April, 1864, the President, Monsieur Marbeau, thus replies to objections made to the crèches:

"The crèche furnishes work instead of alms, aids without humiliating, elevates in aiding, effects a present and future good, and can do harm to none. Why, then, is the system so slow in taking root in Paris, where it commenced, and where it is most needed? It is because people have made objections, founded upon false hypotheses, and contrary to the nature of things. They still exist after twenty years, notwithstanding the facts to the contrary. Let us endeavor, as soon as possible, to remove these objections to the extension of this good work.

"1st objection. The workwoman who becomes a mother should think of nothing besides her infant and her household.—When the husband's earnings are sufficient, and he is temperate, this is possible; but when he dies, or is sick, or has deserted his post, must not the wife provide for all? Labor is essential for both sexes, and the habit of industry should be inculcated upon children, especially those of the laboring classes.

"2d objection. The gathering together of very young children is dangerous.—The care taken to remove any sick child, to secure ventilation and cleanliness, obviates every difficulty; and physicians have already shown that sixty children, or even a larger number, can be assembled without inconvenience even to the youngest. Wholesome nourishment and tender care invigorate the most feeble. Sister Rosalie takes pride in exhibiting her little *sauvés;* a bouillon and a few drops of wine have performed the miracle.

"3d objection. The crèche separates the mother from the child. —No, it is her work which separates her. The crèche prevents this separation every day, and when it does occur, it is only for three or four hours, and prevents the real separation which results from sending the child to a distant nurse, and in many cases prevents its entire abandonment.

"4th objection. The crèche tends to weaken the affection of the mother for the child.—Those who reason thus neither comprehend maternal love, nor have witnessed what may constantly be seen at the crèche. Maternal love is the strongest and most enduring affection of the human heart. The mother brings her child in the early morning, nurses it, and places it in its cradle, commends it to the care of its guardian, bestows a kiss upon it, and hastens to her work, not, however, without casting many a look behind. When she leaves the work-shop at noon, she returns to nurse her child, and remains with it until the hour for work begins. If her labor permit, she may return a second and even a third time. When the day's labor is over, she hastens to it, nurses it, and carries it home. On the morrow, however rude the weather, however long the walk or rough the road, she repeats the same process, and thus it goes on during fourteen or fifteen months. What love! what devotion! Has the crèche, then, the advantage of helping other than good mothers? Yes. The bad mothers have abandoned their children to free themselves from the cost, the sacrifices, and the thousand attendant cares. Public charity undertakes to dispose of all children on the single condition that the parents shall have nothing more to do with them. The true mother accepts no such conditions. A smile from the child, the sight of its well-doing and progress, repays her for all her pains. Can this love be estranged by a few hours' absence? Every mother will answer in the negative, and each one of us who can remember his early years will give the same reply.

"5th objection. The crèche weakens the affection of the child for its mother and its family. — It is true that filial love is less strong than the maternal. Affection descends. Filial love, though instinctive also, for its development as well as preservation requires cultivation. The child loves whoever loves and cares for it. It loves its mother most, because she does for it what no one else would be willing to do. Filial love is but the reflex action of maternal love, which is extinguished at the almshouse, becomes lessened with the distant nurse, but at the crèche has not the time to be extinguished or estranged. The mother who should discover such estrangement, would at once withdraw the child, even if she were to suffer the tortures of poverty by so doing. I have seen this happen. Nothing is grander than the struggle of maternal affection with misfortune. We would say to the skeptic, visit the crèche at the hours when the mothers come to nurse their children."

We give below some of the more important regulations for the establishment of crèches, by public authority:

"Children shall receive at the crèches, until the age when they can resort to the "salle d'asile,"* or until they have completed their third year, the physical and moral care suited to their age. They cannot be retained during the night. Weaned children shall be separated as much as possible from the unweaned.

"Each ward must contain at least eight cubic metres of air for each child, and must have windows which can be easily opened for ventilation. Every crèche must have an uncovered area for taking air and exercise.

"No establishment can be opened until the Prefect has inspected the premises, and has satisfied himself that the sanitary conditions above described have been complied with. The order granting such permission shall specify the number of children to be admitted.

"The care of the crèches shall be exclusively confided to females, and no one shall take such charge unless she shall be twenty-one years of age, and unless she shall furnish a certificate of capacity, signed by two well-known ladies, and endorsed by the mayor and the minister of the parish. A recommendation from the superior of a religious order will be received instead of the above.

"The crèches shall be visited daily by a physician. No child who is not healthy, or who has not been vaccinated, or whose parents are not willing that it should be vaccinated, can be admitted.

"These regulations apply to all establishments, whether public institutions or those sustained by private charity."

The following rules apply to the *crèches approuvées*, or those of the latter class:

* To be described hereafter.

"Every crèche for which the sanction of the Empress is desired, should forward a request to the Minister of the Interior, through the Prefect, with the sanction of the Municipal Council. There shall be enclosed two copies of the by-laws, the last two reports of the society, the accounts of the past year, a statement of the dimensions of the wards and the number of children accommodated. Every institution thus approved shall be managed by a Board consisting of the two sexes. The mayor and the curate shall be *ex-officio* members of the Board. A record shall be kept of the name, age, time of admission, physical state of each child, with name and address of parents; also, number of children admitted each day, with observations of physician, inspectors, or visitors. Each crèche shall have one attendant for every six nursing children, and one for every twelve children between the ages of twelve and eighteen months, none of whom shall be allowed to receive compensation from the parents. Every mother admitted shall agree to nurse her infant during the day; any mother of immoral character may be excluded. The amount to be paid for each child shall be fixed by the Board of Managers, and shall be founded upon the rate of wages paid in the town.

"The crèches shall be open to the inspection of the public. Before the 31st of March in each year the President of the Board shall enclose to the Prefect an annual report, stating receipts and expenses, and a general account of the affairs of the institution. After approval by the Prefect, it shall be by him transmitted to the Minister of the Interior. Any approved crèche may receive aid from government, on application to the Minister of the Interior, with approval of the Empress."

In several crèches experiments have been made in furnishing employment to the children. In some cases, old papers and letters are given to the oldest at certain times of the day, and they occupy themselves in tearing them up into very small pieces, with which pillows are stuffed for the use of the sick. The children take great pleasure in the process, and it is found to be an excellent expedient to keep them quiet and contented.

CHAPTER XXI.

SALLES D'ASILE.

THE salle d'asile is a kind of refuge, resembling, in many respects, the crèche, but intended for the reception of children between the ages of two and six years. It has also some of the features of a primary school, and for that reason has been placed under the direction of the Minister of Public Instruction. The conception of the institution is attributed to the pastor Oberlin, who made the first trial of the plan at the commencement of the present century. His idea seems to have been to gather around him the children of the poor peasants during the day, and to give them useful instruction, thereby leaving the parents to gain their living in following their usual occupations. The plan was soon adopted in England, and in 1826 Mons. Cochin founded the first of the kind in France, placing it in the midst of the poor population of the Faubourg St. Marcel, at Paris. Other establishments succeeded in Paris and other large towns, until now they have become general. The salles d'asile are of two kinds, public and private, and are subjected to regulations very similar to those heretofore described for the crèches. The decree of the Minister authorizing their organization is dated March 31, 1853, and the principal conditions are as follows:

"The children shall be taught the first principles of religion, reading, writing, mental arithmetic, and linear drawing; also, such useful knowledge as is appropriate to their age, suitable handiwork, sacred hymns and psalms, and shall also enjoy bodily exercise. Instruction on moral points shall not exceed ten or fifteen minutes at any one time, and shall always be varied by bodily exercise. In the Catholic establishments, the religious instruction shall be under the direction of the bishop. In those belonging to other denominations recognized by the government, religious instruction shall be given under the direction of the parish ministers. Every salle shall be on the ground floor, and shall be well lighted and ventilated. In each Catholic asile there shall be a crucifix, and an image of the virgin; also, a portrait of the Empress, the patroness of the institution. The title of 'asile modele' may be conferred on such establishments as may particularly excel in their internal arrangements and general management. Every child on entrance must have the certificate of the physician that it has no contagious disease, and that it has been vaccinated. Those children are admitted gratuitously whose parents are unable to pay the monthly subscription. The mayor, with the ministers of the various churches, shall prepare a list of the children to be admitted gratuitously, which list shall be submitted for approval to the Municipal Council."

SUPERVISION.

Independently of the Committee for the Superintendence of Schools, there may be established in each town, and in each ward of Paris where there are asiles, a local Board of Patronesses, who shall be selected by the Prefect. The curate of the parish shall be a member of this Board, and the mayor shall be President. This committee shall be charged with the collection of the charitable offerings for the institution, shall see that the funds supplied by the town, the Department, or the State, are properly applied, and they shall also deliberate upon all questions which may be thought worthy the attention of the committee. They shall meet at least once in each month. One or more physicians, selected by the mayor, shall visit the salles once each week, and shall make a record of each visit, with his prescriptions. The Minister of Public Instruction may appoint a female inspector for the salles, who shall be paid from the public funds.

There are many other details respecting the organization of the Central Board of Management at Paris, the appointment and qualification of teachers, which it would be superfluous to introduce in this place. The asiles are opened, from March till November, from 7 A. M. till 7 P. M., and from November to March, from 8 A. M. till 8 P. M. They are closed on Sundays, and at All Saints, Christmas, New Year's, Ascension, and Assumption days.

If children are not taken away at the proper time, they are conducted home by a competent person. If the parents, after due notice, habitually fail to take their children at the proper time, they are excluded from the asile by an order of the mayor on recommendation of the local Board. When a child is brought to the asile, the Directress explains to the parents the manner in which it should be treated at home in regard to food and cleanliness. Each child is provided with a little lunch-basket, a sponge and drinking-cup, and the Directress inspects the provisions brought, and satisfies herself as to their quantity and quality. If a child is ill on arrival at the asile, it is not received. If it becomes ill during the day, it is carried home, or, in case of emergency, to a physician. If a child becomes fatigued, it is allowed to recline on a bed or hammock, or is cared for in the Directress's apartment. When a child has been frequently absent, without known cause, the Directress informs herself of such cause, and acquaints the committee therewith. No child is subjected to corporeal punishment, and in case reprimand be necessary, it is ordered that it be done with gentleness.

"No other punishment than the following can be inflicted, viz., to stand upright for ten minutes while the others are seated, to forbid their working or studying with the others, and to turn their backs upon their companions. Little presents and marks of approbation may be given as rewards for good conduct, and a certain number of good marks may entitle a child to some useful present. Suitable religious instruction shall be given, with illustrations from the Bible; also, examples of piety and charity shall be quoted, and illustrated by little pictures and images. The moral teaching shall be such as will tend to inspire the child with a profound love of God, gratitude to the Emperor and their august patroness the Empress; to fulfil their duties towards parents and superiors, and to make them gentle, courteous, and kind to each other. Reading lessons shall consist in teaching the vowels, consonants, the alphabet, the accents of punctuation, syllables, and words. Instruction in writing shall be confined to copying letters of the alphabet on the slate. They shall be instructed in simple numeration, addition, and subtraction, illustrated with counters; the multiplication table in rhyme, and explanation of weights and measures illustrated with solid figures or pictures. Instruction in linear drawing shall consist in representing the most simple geometrical figures, and little pictures. Simple sewing and knitting shall be taught; also, the first principles of vocal music. Lessons and exercises shall be begun and ended with a short prayer. The exercise shall consist in marching and calisthenic movements in the school-room, yard, or garden, and games suitable to the age shall be allowed at all times under the eye of the Directress. The children's minds shall not be burdened with the committal to memory of dialogues and dramatic scenes. The Directress shall attend carefully to the physical, moral, and intellectual wants of the children, to their language and habits during the day, and shall also see that their assistants set a good example in all these particulars."

Minute directions are given as to the kind and arrangement of furniture, and other details regarding the comfort of the pupils. The following regulations are contained in an order of the government, dated August 5, 1859:

"On their arrival at the asile, the children shall be assembled in the open area, if the weather permits, where they shall be allowed to amuse themselves under the eye of the Directress or her assistant. At a quarter before ten the children shall enter the school-room, and arrange themselves in their seats. At ten o'clock they shall be taught reading; from a quarter after ten to a quarter before eleven they shall engage in manual employments, suitable to their age and sex. At a quarter before eleven they shall range themselves upon the platform. From eleven till a quarter after eleven, they shall be taught mental arithmetic, with the aid of counters. A half-hour shall then be given to religious instruction, to be concluded by the chanting of prayers and hymns. At twelve the children shall dine. At half-past twelve they shall be conducted to the wash-room, where the attendants shall wash their faces and hands. From one till two they shall be allowed to play in the area. At a quarter after two they shall resume their seats and manual employment. At a quarter before three they shall place themselves on the platform, and at three the Directress shall relate little stories from which some good moral can be drawn. At a quarter after three she shall give them explanation on some point of useful knowledge. At half-past three they shall sing in chorus. At a quarter before four they shall descend from the platform. At four they shall take lunch, and then shall return to their plays until the hour of closing."

In 1860, there were in France about 2,700 salles d'asile, two-thirds of them being public, and one-third private establishments. They were frequented by 250,000 children; and 1,700 are directed by Sisters of some religious order, while 1,000 are under the charge of lay-women. About three-fourths of the children are admitted gratuitously. Besides 2,700 directresses, there are 1,400 assistant teachers, and 1,500 attendants. As the asiles belong to the towns, they receive but little aid from government. The last annual appropriation for the purpose was 380,000 francs.

CHAPTER XXII.

ENFANTS ASSISTÉS (FOUNDLINGS).

THE subject of the treatment of abandoned children has long occupied a great share of public attention in France, and few matters pertaining to the administration of public charity have excited as much interest, or have given rise to such discussions and differences of opinion. The various administrations have been much perplexed as to the proper course to be followed, and have for centuries vainly struggled against an evil which has been constantly on the increase. The alternative has been to withhold aid and allow children to perish who might be cruelly forsaken by their parents; or, by taking an opposite course, to encourage a great and growing evil, thereby creating a serious drain upon the resources of the State. Among the first institutions erected for foundlings was that established at Montpelier, in 1070, by Fathers of the Order of the Holy Spirit. In 1158 a tour was placed in the hospital of that order at Marseilles, and their example was soon followed at Aix and Toulon. In 1362 a brotherhood was organized in Paris, for the benefit of neglected children, under the direction of the bishop, and the Hospital du St. Esprit was opened for their reception. The Hotel Dieu, at Lyons, opened its doors for the same class in 1523.

St. Vincent de Paule, who became so distinguished for his charitable labors in the 17th century, seems to have been the first to influence the public authorities to acknowledge the civil existence of the foundlings, and for this service he is at the present day regarded as their patron saint and special benefactor. He was not, as has been frequently stated, the founder of the first hospital for abandoned children, but he was the means of promoting great ameliorations in those already existing, by entrusting them to the care of Sisters of Charity, belonging to an admirable society, now bearing his name, and which was the conception of his friend and coadjutor, Madame Le Gras. Before his day, the foundlings were exposed in the church porches and public squares, as they anciently were exposed at Rome, and those who survived the exposure were sold to the first comer. In the 17th century, according to a report of the keeper of the Chatelet, at that time the great prison of the capital, three or four hundred children were annually turned into the streets from that establishment. From thence they were gathered into a miserable lodging in the Rue St. Landry, where they received a nominal care from a poor widow, acting under the authority of the chapter of the church of Notre Dame.* As the establishment had no support but what could be obtained from private sources, the inmates were exposed to every kind of hardship and privation, and about one-fourth of the number died. It is stated by several authors, that the attendants,

* Several of these children were carried daily to the doors of the church, and exhibited by the Sisters of Charity, with the cry, "Help these poor foundlings!"

when worried by the cries of the children, often gave drugs enough to produce death. Those who escaped death were often sold at twenty sous each, or were given to persons engaged in the infamous traffic of buying and selling children. "Sometimes," says Mons. Collet, "the children were put to nurse with women laboring under diseases which contaminated their milk, and thus brought about speedy death. Others were sacrificed in the magical operations peculiar to that day, or for the purpose of obtaining blood baths, which were sometimes administered as a curative agent." "It seemed," says Mons. Capefigue, "as if these poor beings were condemned to death at their birth; the few who survived grew up without means, having no sentiments of virtue or industry, and helped to swell the ranks of beggars and abandoned women who infested Paris. Although in exceptional cases efforts had been made for the relief of foundlings,* they were held in such disrepute, that they were not considered as entitled to the protection of government." An edict published by Charles VII., in 1415, has the following clause:

"In giving alms to foundlings, it might happen there would be so many that many people would abandon them, and would have less difficulty in doing so, when they see such bastard children are better cared for without charge or solicitude to themselves."

In 1536, the Hospital des Enfants Dieu, since called Enfants Rouges, was founded by Francis I., for children whose parents had died at the Hotel Dieu, but from that institution,

* Among others, by John of Menlan, bishop of Paris, who built the Hospital du St. Esprit, on the Place du Grève, in 1363; also, by Olivier de La Trau, at Montpelier and St. Mainbœuf, at Angers.

as well as from others, illegitimate children were excluded by law. Matters stood thus in regard to this class, until St. Vincent de Paule, by his eloquence and active sympathy, roused the public conscience, and finally succeeded in obtaining government aid and recognition for the class whose cause he had pleaded. Under his auspices a few children were gathered in a house in the Faubourg St. Victor, which being soon filled, they were transferred to the Chateau de Bicetre, which was set apart for that object by the king. This site having been found too exposed, they were transferred to the Hospital St. Lazare; from thence, in 1672, to the cité, and one hundred years later, to a large and magnificent building constructed for the purpose in the Parvis Notre Dame. Here they remained until the Revolution, during which the ancient abbey of Port Royal, in the Rue Royal, and the Maison de L'Oratoire, were assigned to their use. The first of these is now used for a lying-in hospital, and the last for the foundlings. Liberal gifts were bestowed for the object by Louis XIII., Anne of Austria, and Louis XIV. By an edict of the latter king, dated in 1670, the foundling hospital was placed on the same footing as the other hospitals of Paris. He says: "Considering it as a Christian duty to care for these children, whose feebleness and misfortune make them worthy of compassion; and further than this, their preservation is an advantage, because they may be useful in the country's service." In comparing this edict with that of Charles, issued two and a half centuries earlier, the change in public sentiment may be seen, and to St. Vincent de Paule, more than to any one else, must be ascribed the merit of having aroused the public conscience to a sense of the common obligations of humanity. By various statutes of Parliament, the local seignors, in the Provinces, were obliged to care for all abandoned children in their respective territories; but after the establishment of a special hospital for their reception in Paris, the seigneurs and small towns made no scruple of sending all children of that class to the new institution. As the transit was made at all seasons and in all weathers, the mortality was frightful, and the burden on the hospital soon became too great to be borne.* A decree of the Royal Council, dated Jan. 10, 1779, says: "His majesty is informed that more than 2,000 children are yearly brought to the foundling hospital at Paris, from distant provinces. These children, which paternal care at home can with difficulty guard against the dangers peculiar to this tender age, are placed at all seasons in charge of public carriers, who, absorbed with other interests, are obliged to spend a long time on the journey. It thus happens that these unfortunate victims to their parents' cruelty suffer so much from the journey, that nearly nine-tenths of the whole number perish before they are three months old." The decree adds in conclusion:

"His majesty sees with regret that the number of foundlings increases daily, and that the majority are born in legitimate wedlock; so that the institutions, originally established to prevent the crime which shame might lead the mother to perpetrate, are becom-

* The number of foundlings in 1680 was 800; in 1740, 3,140; in 1750, 3,789; in 1760, 5,032; in 1770, 6,918. The opponents of St. Vincent de Paule made use of these facts, even during his life, as an argument against his work.

ing by degrees a convenience for criminal indifference on the part of parents. By such an abuse the public treasury is burdened, and in the large towns the great increase of these children is out of all proportion to the funds and provision made for their benefit."

By this decree a fine of 1,000 livres was imposed on any one who should bring a child to Paris for the purpose of abandonment. It was ordered that all such foundlings should be carried to the nearest hospital, and if such hospital had not the necessary means, the king would provide for them for the first year, and would see that the funds were supplied after that period. It does not appear that this and other stringent measures taken tended to lessen the evil complained of, and at the present time, with the increased facilities for travel and transportation, it is shown that Paris, with less than one-twentieth of the population, contains about one-fifth of all the abandoned children of France.*

*The number of foundlings at the hospital in Paris, on the 31st Dec., 1864, was 107; number received during the year, 3,786; but, adding 703 who returned, the whole number was 4,489. 4,061 were placed in the country or left. The number of foundlings in the country, and in charge of the administration, was 18,071. If to these are added past inmates of the hospital, from twelve to twenty-one years of age, for which no board is paid, the whole number of children in charge of the administration on the 31st Dec., 1864, was 23,228. Of the 3,786 received during the year, 499 were legitimate, 3,201 were illegitimate, and eighty-six were unknown. Of the illegitimate, the parents of 382 were known, and 2,819 were unknown. 1,061 were born at residence of the mother; 872 were born at residence of the midwives; 1,785 were born at the hospitals, and sixty-eight were found in the streets. 421, or 9.17 per cent. died in the hospital, whereas in 1858, 19.91 died, showing a diminution of more than one-half in a period of seven years.

The amount asked for to meet the expenses of this department for the present year (1866) is 2,416,200 francs.

CHAPTER XXIII.

ABANDONED CHILDREN.

IT is well known that during the Revolution not only was no effort made to discourage the practice of abandoning children, but a direct premium was held out for its encouragement. By a law enacted in 1790, foundlings were declared to be *Enfants de la Patrie* (children of the State), and their support was declared to be a public duty. Later, or in 1793, an act was passed, making an appropriation for the support of all children born of poor parents, and in aid of all young women *enceinte*, with a guaranty that their secret should be kept. By this decree the children thus born were to be called "Enfants Naturels de la Patrie." This designation appears in several subsequent acts, but was lost sight of during the Consulate. Such legislation tended, of course, to promote libertinism and vice among the poorer classes, but, according to Mons. Dupin, the statute had little practical effect. An honest shame prevented most young women from availing themselves of it, and the vicious alone were willing to accept the boon. Of the latter class, some promised to resume their evil courses, while others, thinking their services too little remunerated, threatened that they would become sterile. Such a vicious system could not long be tolerated, and soon ceased from its absurdity. On the

27th Frimaire of the year 5, the Directory passed a law by which foundlings should be received and cared for in all the hospitals and hospices of the Republic, and when any hospital had not sufficient funds to meet the expenses caused by their reception, the necessary amount should be furnished by the public treasury. It was also provided that such children should remain under care of the authorities until they were of age or apprenticed, and penalties were inflicted on any person who should leave a child at any other hospice than that nearest to its birthplace. Permission was given to place foundlings in families, and that nurses or persons having charge of them should receive eighteen francs for the first nine months, and fifty francs when the child should attain the age of twelve, the allowance for the intermediate years to vary according to the locality, and to be fixed by the authorities of the various Departments. By an act passed in the year 13, the charge and education of foundlings were given to the General Administration of Hospices.

No complete system for the care of foundlings was adopted until the passage of the act of Napoleon in the year 1811, upon which the whole system of the present day is mainly based.

The principal provisions of the act are the following:

Children who shall be considered at the public charge: 1st, foundlings (*Enfants Trouvés*); 2d, abandoned children (*Enfants Abandonnés*); 3d, destitute orphans (*Orphelius Pauvres*).

FOUNDLINGS.

Foundlings are children belonging to unknown parents, found exposed in any situation whatever, or carried to the hospices opened for their reception. In each hospice destined for such, there shall be a box (*tour*) for their reception. In each arrondissement of Paris there shall be one hospice where foundlings can be received. A daily register shall be kept, designating sex, age, and any natural marks (*langes*) which may serve to identify them.

ABANDONED CHILDREN.

Abandoned children are the offspring of parents who are known, and who have been cared for by such parents or others until a certain age, and have then been forsaken, without it being known where such parents or guardians reside.

ORPHANS.

Orphans are those who have neither father nor mother, nor means of subsistence.

On the arrival of the child at the hospice, the proper officer shall make a record of the fact, with all circumstances relating to its exposure, and shall give it a name, if one has not already been given by the civil officer. A Christian name and surname shall be given. In selecting the surname, the common rules and usages shall be followed, and the child shall be baptized and reared in the Catholic Church, with certain authorized exceptions. No name shall be given which is known to belong to any existing family.* It should be sought in the history, or in certain circumstances surrounding the child, or in his conformation, features, complexion, country, the place where found; always discarding any name which might be considered indecent, ridiculous, or which may serve to remind others in after years that its bearer is a foundling.

Children recently born shall be put out to nurse as soon as possible after arrival, and shall in the mean time be fed by hired nurses residing in the hospice.

When sent out to nurse, they shall be provided with an outfit, and shall remain until the age of six years.

At the age of six they shall, as far as possible, be placed in the families of farmers and mechanics. The price paid for their maintenance shall be diminished each year until the age of twelve, at which period all males shall be placed at the disposal of the Minister of Marine. Children who cannot be placed as above, on account of lameness or infirmity, shall be reared in the hospice, and shall be placed in the work-shops, at labor suitable to their age. 4,000,000 francs are appropriated annually towards the payment of nurses and board of children in families. If this sum shall be insufficient, the deficiency shall be met from the income of the hospice, or by a tax levied upon the town. Monthly payments shall be made to nurses on presentation of a certificate of the Mayor, who shall testify to having seen the child dur-

* These regulations cannot be too strictly followed in this country, where the most honored names are given to children found in the streets or on door-steps.

ing the month. The General Administration of Hospitals shall cause each child to be visited at least twice yearly, either by a special visitor, or by a physician or surgeon.

Foundlings and abandoned children are placed in charge of the General Administration of Hospitals; one member of that administration shall have the special charge of this department. Such children, educated at the charge of the State, shall be placed entirely at its disposal; and the charge of the administration shall cease whenever the Minister of Marine shall assume such charge. Children not taken by the State shall, after completing their twelfth year, be apprenticed, as far as possible, boys with farmers and mechanics, girls with families, work-women, or in work-shops and manufactories. The articles of apprenticeship shall not stipulate for any particular sum, in favor of either master or apprentice, but shall guarantee to the master the services of the apprentice until his twenty-first year, and to the apprentice board and clothing. Should the apprentice be drawn by conscription for the army, the apprenticeship shall cease.

Parents may reclaim their children on payment of all expenses incurred for them by the administration, but this right shall cease when the State shall have disposed of the child.

Any person who shall leave a child exposed in a solitary place, or shall have given the order to do so, if the order is executed, shall be condemned to imprisonment from six months to two years, and shall pay a fine of from 16 to 200 francs. If, by the exposure, the child become mutilated or injured, such injury shall be considered as having been caused by the person so exposing it; and if death ensues, the crime shall be considered murder. Any person abandoning a child in a place not considered solitary, shall be imprisoned from three months to one year, and shall pay a fine of from 16 to 100 francs.

Much discussion has taken place of late years as to the mode of admission to foundling hospitals. The principal difference of opinion is in regard to the continuance of the *tour* * or turn-cradle, a mode of admission borrowed from Italy, where it had been in use since the eighth century.

Those who argue in favor of the old system, lay much stress upon the temptations to which mothers are exposed when such an institution is closed to them. They state that in those departments where the tours have been suppressed, and only a single hospice opened, the health and even the life of the children are often sacrificed, owing to the great distances which it is necessary to transport them before finding a shelter. They ask that the abuses of the *tour* shall be guarded against, but not that it shall be suppressed.

The opponents of the system argue that its continuance, by the secrecy permitted, tends to increase a great public evil. As the hospices had been open to all, the plan had operated as an encouragement to libertinage, by the means offered for concealing its results. The children thus disposed of are often the fruit of legitimate marriages, and are abandoned by their parents from lack of maternal affection, or on account

* The tour is a wooden box or cradle fixed on a pivot. The parent places the child in the cradle, and turns it inwards. The attendant is warned by the ringing of a bell attached to the apparatus, and the parent escapes without being recognized.

of difficulty in providing for their wants. These children lose caste, and are ever after the objects of an unjust obloquy; and the administration, by encouraging such a system, becomes an accomplice in perpetuating a great evil. Monsieur Pastoret, in a report to the administration in 1816, says:

"In former times none but illegitimate children were brought to the hospital; by and by came legitimate children, the parents proving false to every duty, and thus stamping on their offspring the stain of bastardy, and depriving them of the advantages accompanying a legitimate birth. From the year 1804 to 1813, 45,921 children were received, 4,332, or about one-tenth of them, being legitimate. The proportions necessarily vary according to circumstances. In years of scarcity, or in manufacturing towns when there is a want of work, there are always those who, already burdened with cares and expenses, are willing to rid themselves of the burden of the new-born child, and avail themselves of the *tour*. Although such an abandonment cannot be justified, there are cases where the crime may be attended with extenuating circumstances. A poor workman, for instance, is left with the care of a new-born child, and finds it impossible to obtain a proper person to take charge of it. Can he give up his daily employment, which furnishes the means of living, in order to care for it himself? The hospital is his only resort, and yet it should be his last. The administration could step in here, and, with the knowledge of the facts, aid the poor man by its counsels and pecuniary aid. The *tour* in such a case can give no advice or information, and is only an evil."

From a report made by a commission acting under the authority of the Minister of the Interior in 1860, it appears that there remained only five tours in France, or one in each of the following towns: Marseilles, Quimper, Evreux, Paris, and Rouen. Two of these *tours* were temporary, and that in Paris was guarded (surveillé*), so that in the opinion of the commission the system may be considered as condemned by experience.

"By its encouragements, its promises to shield from punishment, it inculcates contempt for the most sacred laws, and tends directly to the destruction of family ties. France is not niggard of her resources; but can any statesman hesitate between that blind charity which encourages vice as well as misfortune, and that other method which seeks light in order to bestow more wisely?"

In reply to the assertion that the suppression of the *tour* will lead to the increase of the crime of infanticide, the commission state that no such conclusion can be drawn from the experience of past years. Other crimes have increased in greater proportion than that of infanticide. From 1826 to 1858, the number of cases of parricide had nearly doubled (9 to 17), while rapes and kindred crimes had nearly quadrupled (273 to 1,022). From 1826 to 1832, there was one case of infanticide in 10,274 births; from 1847 to 1853, there was one case in 5,718 births. In the Departments, the suppression or diminution of the *tours* has seemed to exercise very little influence upon the number of cases of this crime. The cases have been more numerous in the country and small

* This surveillance is performed by special agents, who require persons bringing children to declare the name and residence of the parents, and to give such other information as may be desired.

towns than in the great centres of population, where errors in living are more easily concealed. The number of abandoned children in France for the last fifty years has steadily decreased. The number in 1826 was 31,840, whereas in 1853 the number was only 22,066. This diminution is attributed to the suppression of *tours*, and to the system of temporary aid to mothers hereafter described.

As to the risks incurred by the transportation of very young children to the Departmental Hospice, the facilities of travel, and especially those offered by railroads, have removed all danger. Admission to the hospices are not indiscriminately given, but are regulated by a Board, which in Paris consists of the General Director of the administration, some other officials connected with the institution, and the Lady Superior in charge. It is not necessary to carry the child to the hospital before obtaining admission, and it often happens that parents are dissuaded from abandoning their children by the kind offices and advice of the officials.

CHAPTER XXIV.

ABANDONED CHILDREN, CONTINUED.

THE number of foundlings and abandoned children in the various public institutions in 1859, at home and in the colonies, was 76,520, viz.:

Foundlings, boys, ...	18,937
" girls, ...	20,071
Abandoned children, boys, ...	15,131
" " girls, . . .	14,640
Orphans, boys, ...	4,020
" girls, ...	3,721
	76,520

Of these there were in the hospices, . .	3,395
In the country, ...	72,368
In the colonies and orphan asylums, . .	757
	76,520

In 1849, the number of children of the above classes was 92,647; showing a diminution in ten years of 16,127.

A very gratifying result, ascribed principally to the system of temporary aid to mothers. Another result, not less gratifying, is the diminution in the rate of mortality among the children. The number of deaths during these ten years, among children in the public establishments of France, was 56.99 in every 100; while the rate among those receiving temporary aid at home was but 29.56. The same results have been remarked in Paris. In 1860, the General Director of Assistance Publique furnished the following table, with an expression of regret, that, with all the care in treatment, and various ameliorations in the condition of the foundlings, the rate of mortality had not diminished as much as had been expected in the hospitals. From 1839 to 1850, a period of twenty years, there were—

Admitted from one day to ten days old,	48,525	
Died in first ten days, ...		5,372
" ten days to one year old, . . .		21,747
" from one to two years, ...		3,751
Total deaths, ...		30,870

During the same years, the number of children sent to the care of nurses was as follows:

From one day to ten days old, . .	24,169	
Died in one to ten days, ...		489
" from ten days to one year, ...		6,692
Total,.		7,181

The average mortality of children placed with nurses, during twenty years, for the first ten days, was only 2.02, while the rate among children of the same age in the hospital was 11.07; a difference in favor of the former of 9.05. The difference, as already stated, during the first year, exhibits a still stronger contrast, being 26.17 in favor of the first-named class. Although some of the causes of this disparity were evident, such as the feeble condition of children when abandoned, nursing by hand, &c., the administration appointed a special committee to investigate the subject, and to suggest such precautions as they might think expedient. A report was submitted by Dr. Cullerier, and among the various causes of mortality, the following were given: Want of mother's milk; lying too long in a horizontal position; bad state of system on entrance; the bad effect resulting from the regulation requiring the mother to retain the child at her side until her discharge; the custom, now obsolete, of keeping the child in the nursery after vaccination, until healing of the pustule; the delay before admission, on account of legal formalities; insalubrity and smallness of wards, and insufficiency of number of nurses.

The precautionary measures recommended were: The removal of waterproof cloths between the sheet and mattresses, as well as mattresses of cradles; substitution of fine for coarse linen next the skin; limitation of number, no ward to contain more than eighty-five children; increase of number of attendants in department of weaned children; substitution of roasted for boiled meats; enlargement and improvement of wards; country nurses not to be replaced by unmarried nurses belonging to Paris, but goats' milk to be given in preference; increase of salary to nurses; time of sojourn of nurses to be determined by physician; no one having milk more than nine months old to be employed; to increase facilities of transportation, giving children passage in second-class cars.

In regard to vaccination, the committee believe there is no objection to vaccinating the child a very few days after birth, as experience has proved it to be the safer plan, on account of the prevalence of the varioloid in the hospitals, where it is taken by the youngest inmates. It is safest to send children into the country during the first four days succeeding their vaccination, or after the twelfth day. By an order of the administration, issued in 1852, a sufficient number of physicians must be attached to the district of each inspector, to whom they are required to report upon all subjects affecting the welfare of the children. They select nurses, none of whom should be under twenty or more than forty years of age.* For attendance on children less than one year old, the physician receives six francs; for those between one and two, four francs; and for those between two and twelve, three francs. Two francs are allowed for each successful case of vaccination. Further than this, the physician, in connection with the inspector, has the supervision of the children until they are twenty-one years old, and in case of their illness has an allowance of one franc for each visit, with cost of medicine. Helpless and idiotic children are now placed at board in the country, like the others, and very little difficulty is experienced in finding suitable situations.

* In some of the large towns, where many nurses are required, there is a class of men called "*meneurs*," whose duty it is to search for nurses, bring them to the hospice, return them to their homes, and see that they are regularly paid.

CHAPTER XXV.

ABANDONED CHILDREN, CONTINUED.

ON arrival at the hospital, children are baptized, unless proof is afforded that the rite has been already performed. As soon as age and health permit, they are vaccinated. They are nursed by women residing in the institution. Until their departure for the country, the children are kept in a separate apartment, to which no one has access beside those having them in charge. All employées, under penalty of dismission, are forbidden to give any information contained in the Records, or to reveal the place where any child is sent, excepting to General or Department Inspectors. Children are sent into the country as soon as possible, or as soon as the physician declares it can be done with safety to the child or nurse. In selecting places, preference is given to those lying near principal villages, where easy access can be obtained to churches and schools. Situations are selected as far as possible from the towns from which the children are supposed to have been brought. When possible, brothers and sisters are placed in the same family or village. Upon the neck of each child under four years of age is a collar with a small silver medal,* on which is inscribed a number and the name of the hospice. This collar is removed after the fifth year.

A woman wishing to take charge of children produces a certificate from the mayor of the town, stating whether she is married or single, whether she is in comfortable circumstances,† whether of good moral character, the condition of her dwelling as regards salubrity, and, if she has already received children, whether she has taken proper care of them. If the child is not weaned, the applicant shall furnish a certificate from a physician that she is not *enceinte*, that she is not nursing, or, if so, that her child is in a condition to be weaned, and that her milk is abundant and of good quality. Persons receiving a child shall attend strictly to cleanliness; shall give it a separate bed, and, if the child is young, shall have a fire-fender. When it is not weaned, she shall nurse it until it is twelve months old, unless she shall obtain permission to the contrary. She shall take care of its clothing, shall not entrust her charge to others, nor take another child without permission. Whenever required, she shall exhibit the child, its outfit, and her receipt-book, that she may from time to time be enabled to receive her salary. She shall bring the child to the hospital, if required. If she wishes to renounce the care of it, she shall give eight days' notice of her inten

* To prevent the unauthorized exchange of children, a small silver ring has been substituted for the collar, which was found to be insufficient. This ring bears the name of the hospice from which the child was brought, the year, and a number, and is worn until the sixth year.

† The possession of a cow is one test as to the applicant being in comfortable circumstances.

tion to do so. She shall not allow her charge to wander or beg in the highway, and shall send it to church and the public school. She shall inculcate habits of industry by employments suitable to its age and strength. In case the child elopes, the nurse shall notify the mayor, and shall take all necessary steps to recover it. In case of its death, she shall notify the mayor, who shall record the fact, and inform the administration. When a child is taken from the hospice, the person so receiving it shall receive a memorandum-book, giving the number, name, age, and date of its delivery; the name and residence of those who have taken the child; the duties and obligations imposed upon the latter; the price of board, description of outfit, blank form of certificate of vaccination, decease, and several blank pages for remarks of the Inspector. On arrival at home, the nurse will present the child to the mayor, who will endorse the fact on the memorandum-book, and make a minute of the same on his own records. The administration reserves the right to remove any child under twelve years of age, whenever they shall deem it for the interest of said child. Another shall be given as a substitute, whenever such removal has not been caused by any blame or neglect on the part of the nurse. The price of board shall be, for first year, ten francs per month; second year, eight francs per month; third and fourth years, seven francs per month; fifth, sixth, seventh, eighth, and ninth years, six francs per month; tenth, eleventh, and twelfth years, five francs per month. Extra payments may be made for infirm and helpless children. Extra payment may be paid on production of a certificate certifying to the nurse's fidelity, and that the child has been vaccinated. Nurses who have taken an infant soon after birth, have taken good care of it until the age of twelve, have preserved it from any accidents which might be imputed to carelessness, and have caused it to partake of the first communion, shall receive a gratuity of fifty francs. The same amount shall be given to those farmers or artisans, who, whether having brought them up or not, shall take the children who have attained the age of twelve, and shall agree to teach them some trade or calling. This sum shall be used for clothing the children.

Ten sous per kilometre * shall be allowed to each nurse for travelling expenses in going to and returning from hospitals. A gratuity of four francs shall be given to the physician or midwife for every nurse sent to the hospital by them, when such nurse shall fulfil the necessary conditions. The cost of funeral expenses, for children who die in the hospital or elsewhere, is fixed at five francs. Very minute details are given for the layette or outfit of children from the age of one day to twelve years. All clothing is marked with the hospital stamp, and is forwarded by the administration, as required. Details are given for the treatment of children in sickness by local physicians, and liberty is given to return them to the hospital when the case requires such care as cannot be given at home.

Rules are also furnished for the education of children. They must be sent to the primary school when six years old. They are provided with books, paper, and pens, by the pub-

* Five-eighths of a mile.

lic teachers, for which a small allowance is granted. The salles d'asile are required to receive all foundlings, or children temporarily aided. Children are required to attend church on Sundays, and to learn the catechism. At the age of twelve, children are apprenticed, and cease to be at the public charge. If any child expresses a preference for the naval service, the Inspector shall, with the consent of the administration, place him on board a government ship, or merchant vessel, until the age of sixteen, the captain or owner agreeing to take proper care of his health, morals, &c. At the age of sixteen a new agreement is made; the wages not required for the support of the boy are placed in the nearest savings bank. In each principal town an auxiliary Board is established to look after the foundlings in that locality. This Board consists of the mayor, curate, justice of the peace, and, in the small villages, of the school-teacher. The existence of a single foundling in any town authorizes the organization of such a Board, called a "Committee of Patronage."

A circular from the Minister of the Interior, dated Nov. 2, 1862, says:

"Experience has already proved the utility of such a Board, and that the Inspector, however zealous and devoted to his duties, cannot be always present, while the child requires constant protection. As he is absorbed in other duties, the rules of the central administration are often unheeded; it is desirable to substitute a local supervision, which shall be always present to watch over the interests of both parties.

"This auxiliary Board is eminently fitted to accomplish this end. Experience has proved it, and if in some rare instances it has proved a failure, in others it has met with unexpected success. The essential element of success is that there should be found in the Board no useless element, and that there should only be devoted men, with a design to do good, and finding their reward in the fulfilment of duty. Three or five or seven members are sufficient. Large committees rarely work well. By dividing the responsibility among too many, it ceases to be felt by any, and each member is but too willing to throw the burden on his colleague. Rather than increase the number of the committee, it would be preferable to multiply the number of Boards.

"In the large towns several might be formed, bounded by certain limits; in the smaller towns one would be enough. All the members should take a part in the supervision of the children; they should visit them often, see that patrons and nurses perform their respective duties, give to each encouragement, and good advice, and all necessary information, and report to the Prefect, the Board, or the Inspector, their observations, or such suggestions as they may think proper.

"It is at the time of apprenticeship the local committee can be useful. The subsidy having ceased, the patrons have no longer the same motive to care for the pupils, and it may happen that the child be overtasked, his education and meals neglected, and that he be allowed to lose in the work-shop all hope for future improvement. When restrained by the constant vigilance of the visitor, both master and apprentice will be desirous of fulfilling their respective duties, and the administration will not have to fear those failures which are the common result in the absence of a constant supervision.

"By the correspondence of their various committees, and by their influence, young men who have been brought up in the country can be retained where their strong arms are so much needed."

CHAPTER XXVI.

SOCIÉTÉS DE CHARITÉ MATERNELLE.

THE object of these societies is to aid lying-in women, by providing for their immediate wants, and enabling them afterwards to nurse and care for their children. The first institution of the kind was established in Paris in 1788, under the auspices of Marie Antoinette, by Madame Fougeret. This lady was the daughter of one of the administrators of hospitals, whose sympathies had been much excited by witnessing the sufferings of this class. With the assistance of friends and others, she organized, in the different quarters of Paris, a system of relief for poor families having many children. The relief consisted of an outfit (*layette*) for the new-born child, and a small sum of money for the mother while nursing. As a condition, it was stipulated that the mother, whenever possible, should nurse her infant. The society was abolished during the Revolution, but was again organized, under the patronage of the Empress Marie Louise, by two acts dated respectively May 5th and July 25th, 1810. The society embraced the whole of France, and was governed by a Board, consisting of public dignitaries, and ladies nominated by the Empress. This association was again abolished on the return of the Bourbons, and the Paris society placed on its former footing, with a provision that other towns might adopt a similar organization, with permission of the Minister of the Interior, when they had obtained sufficient subscriptions. In a report made to the King in 1837, Mons. De Gusparin considers this society as one of the best instruments for the diminution of the number of abandoned children. Mons. Dupin also bears testimony to its utility, and says:

> "When a child has lived a year, and its mother has enjoyed its first smile, there is no danger that she will abandon it. Besides this, a bond of interest springs up between the mother and her protectrice, which insures to the former an interest in her future well-being."

The Société de la Maternité gives aid, at the time of confinement, to the woman who, while enceinte, has become a widow, and who has at least one child living; to a woman already having one child, and a husband who is disabled or affected by a chronic disease; to those disabled, having two children living; to those who, with two children already, have twins; to those having already three children living, the eldest under the age of fourteen. A disabled child of fourteen is counted as a young child.

The mother must present herself during the month preceding her confinement to the Director who has charge of her quarter. She must produce a certificate of marriage, another of good moral character, as well as one from the Bureau de Bienfaisance, testifying to her need; the certificate of baptism of her children, and if a widow, the record of her husband's death. If infirm or disabled, the fact should be certified by a physician or surgeon. The applicant must agree to nurse her child, or to feed it by hand. She can claim aid during the month following her confinement.

After these preliminaries the society pays the expenses of the accouchement, furnishes a layette to the child, and a grant of five francs monthly for ten months. Should the mother be sick, the child may be intrusted to a nurse, and three francs more allowed monthly. If the mother dies, the association takes the child in charge, and five francs per month may be allowed for it. The committee of lady visitors in Paris consists of forty-eight members, and meets once each month to decide upon admissions, and amount of aid to be given. Each lady visitor has charge of a certain section. She is to investigate the character and claims of applicants, and to exercise a general supervision of the persons aided.

This association relieves 800 families annually, and receives from government 40,000 francs, and from the city of Paris 6,000 francs. The remainder of the sum necessary for its support is made up by individual subscriptions, amounting to 10,000 francs annually.

CHAPTER XXVII.

BUREAUX DES NOURRICES.

THIS association has been formed for the purpose of procuring nurses. The number of mothers in large cities, and especially in Paris, who are unable to nurse their own children, is very large, and the demand has been so great that a regular traffic has long been carried on by mercenary persons, much to the detriment of nurses as well as of their employées. To remedy abuses, and for the protection of the nurses, government has taken the subject under its own control, and has adopted the present system. As far back as the fourteenth century, laws were enacted, entrusting the business of procuring nurses to privileged persons, who were subject to certain restrictions, and amenable to punishment for abuses.

There existed formerly in Paris an association under the name of "Recommandeurs," who enjoyed the monopoly of procuring nurses from the provinces by agents of their own, called "Meneurs," men generally of little intelligence and less morality. By means of an understanding with the "Sages femmes," they succeeded in organizing private establishments, which eclipsed the public bureaux, and received the support of some of the noted *accoucheurs* of the day. As the chances for profit were great, and limited only by the public demand, great abuses were practised, and nurses were bought and sold like merchandise. Women of attractive appearance, called, in the language of the day, *voyageuses*, introduced themselves to parents, who, deceived by their good looks, did not hesitate to commit their children to their care. The child passed from her hands to a second, and often to a third person, greatly to the injury of its health, and often at the cost of life.*

The foundation of the bureau at Paris dates from the year 1769, and that at Lyons was organized by letters patent in 1780. The act of 1806 provides for the mode of collecting nurses' wages. In the year 9 of the Revolution, the bureau was placed under the administration of hospitals. By an act of 1849, the whole subject was placed under the administration of Bienfaisance Publique, where it now remains. A sub-inspector is appointed for each arrondissement, who is charged with the care of all children within his district. He is aided by physicians, whose duty it is to give all needful care to nurses as well as children. Under the inspector there is a female superintendent of nurses, nominated by himself, whose duty is to attend to the transportation of children sent into the country by the administration. She receives the observations of the mayors and curates, as well as complaints of nurses, settles minor disputes, referring the more impor-

* These manœuvres were so well understood by the country people that they nicknamed the business "Traité des petits blancs," which might be translated "Slave-trade of little whites." The race of *meneurs* is not extinct, as a woman named Laumain was condemned for the crime in July, 1864.

tant to the administration. She is required to visit every child in her district at least once in two months, to correspond with the General Director on all subjects respecting her duties, and to transmit quarterly reports of her doings. She also provides for the wants of the children, and sees that the nurses are promptly paid. She gives bonds for good behavior, and on assuming her office receives advances amounting to three-fourths of her bonds. Besides a salary of 600 francs, the inspector receives 75 centimes a month for each child placed under his care, though his receipts, however large the number of children, must not exceed 3,500 francs annually. The physicians to the bureau are appointed by the Prefect of the Seine, on the nomination of the General Director. They are allowed 50 centimes per visit to each nurse admitted, and 75 centimes for each nurse and child. They are also allowed two francs for each successful vaccination of a child, if performed within the first three months after it has been placed with the nurse. The physicians are also charged with the selection of the nurses, selecting in preference those who are in comfortable circumstances, and who have an abundance of milk.

The nurse, after being approved by the inspector, goes to Paris, under the direction of the superintendent, and reports herself to the bureau. She should present a certificate of good moral character, that she has weaned her child, has no other infant to nurse, that she is in a position to care properly for her charge, and is the owner of a cradle. While in Paris the nurses are lodged by the administration, and receive an allowance for food. On leaving the city, each hired nurse receives a book containing her name, with that of the child, the date of its birth, and of its reception by her. For each nurse the administration grants two francs for travelling expenses back and forth, and three francs to the superintendent. The sum paid as salary to the nurse is a matter of agreement between herself and the party hiring her, although the administration guarantees only the payment of twelve francs per month, and this guaranty is only given when the child is less than ——— months old, and is then only made for ten months, including the first month, for which parents pay in advance. Before the fifth day of every month, the director addresses to the sub-inspector an account of the sums paid by parents during the preceding month. Every child must be visited at least monthly by the physician, who is bound to report its condition to the inspector. Every fortnight the director sends a report of the names of the nurses and children admitted. To make up deficiencies of receipts and excess of expenditures, the city of Paris makes an annual grant, which varies from year to year. In 1854, the sum granted was 285,000 francs.

CHAPTER XXVIII.

TEMPORARY AID TO MOTHERS.

A SYSTEM of temporary aid has been lately adopted, by which mothers of legitimate or illegitimate children are aided, thereby lessening the temptation to abandonment of their offspring for lack of the means of support. The indiscriminate aid afforded by the Convention, to which allusion has been made, and which had become so burdensome to the State, is now avoided, and such assistance only given as to encourage the mother with her daily work to eke out her existence, and to fulfil those maternal duties which, without aid, she is so sorely tempted to neglect. Many of the Departments have adopted this mode of relief, and the favorable results may be seen by reference to the detailed reports of the commission appointed by the government to investigate the operation of the system. The following are the statistics for the years 1857–1859:

Year.	Admitted to hospitals.	Temporarily aided.	Total.
1857, . .	19,473	6,694	26,167
1858, . . .	17,999	7,723	25,722
1859, . .	16,761	9,173	25,934

showing that while temporary aid was given to about twenty-five per cent. of the mothers in 1857, the proportion had, in 1859, been increased to thirty-five per cent.

This table represents the average number aided in the whole country, while the proportion in some Departments was seventy-six, eighty-four, and even ninety per cent.

Although the number of abandoned children has not sensibly diminished, the results of the experiment have been gratifying in a financial point of view. The expense of maintaining a foundling during the twelve years which it remained under the care of the administration, has been 1,403 francs and thirty centimes, divided as follows:

Maintenance in hospital, . . .	160.84
Outfit, ...	160.16
Salary of nurses, . . .	923.78
Cost of inspection, ...	158.52
	1,403.30

The average cost of each child aided at home during the three years 1857–8–9, after which time it ceases to be at the public charge, is as follows:

For 1st year, . . .	87.12	francs.
For 2d "	76.56	"
For 3d "	69.24	"
	232.92	"

or about one-sixth of the cost of the child received into the hospital.

The commissioners add:

"If the system could be generally adopted, the annual expenses would be 1,700,000 francs, instead of 10,000,000, the present cost. Under present regulations, aid is allowed to the mother by the Prefect, or Sub-Prefect, on the recommendation of an inspector, but with rare exceptions to unmarried women, except in the case of a first child, and then only after she has recognized it according to the forms of law, and when the necessary aid cannot be obtained from those who are legally bound to maintain it. After the name of the child is inscribed upon the register, it is entitled to the supervision of the inspector, just as if it had been admitted to the hospital. If the mother neglects her duties, the allowance is stopped; or if, on account of sickness or other cause, she cannot nurse her infant, it may be placed with a nurse, who then receives the allowance.

"The mother cannot act as nurse for any other child than her own, who, in the mean time, is entitled to gratuitous medical attendance, and in case of death is buried at the public expense. In those departments where aid is given for more than the three first years, it is withdrawn if the circumstances of the mother allow it, or if the child be found begging on the highway. If the mother dies, the allowance is still continued to the child, and appropriated to whoever consents to take it in charge. This system of temporary aid often acts favorably in promoting the marriage of parents of illegitimate children. To encourage such unions, a special grant of from sixty to one hundred francs is made to the mother, and besides, there is an association called Société St. François de Regis, specially devoted to this object."

The commissioners before named say:

"Only cases entitled to sympathy receive the aid of the administration. The child and not the mother is the gainer.* It gains by escaping the dangers of exposure, in securing the devoted care of its mother, and in securing the endearments, the pleasures, and the honor of the family. Let it not be asserted that such a child is more highly favored than the offspring of legitimacy. In the one case, without aid, the child has no prospect but abandonment and death. The other has a father and mother who can afford their care and affection. How can the two be compared?"

Permission is given to aid illegitimate children where there is imminent danger of their abandonment, and where the mother is disposed to continue her maternal duties. Experience has shown that the efficacy of this system of temporary aid depends upon the character and fidelity of those who are called to administer it, and who can give their whole time and energies to the promotion of its interests. This end, it is thought, has been attained under the present organization. The number of inspectors is eighty-seven, embracing many distinguished names experienced in the departments of State, the judiciary, the army, the medical profession, and the business walks of life. The post is rather honorary than otherwise, as the average annual salary is only 2,351 francs, with allowance of travelling expenses. With the exception of the Department of the Seine,† where there is a special organiza-

* The common term by which the recipients have been known, is Filles Mères. In a circular dated May 27, 1856, the Minister of the Interior says that this designation is improper, and, instead of the term, *Secours aux Filles Mères,* recommends the use of the expression, *Secours aux Enfants Nouveaux Nés.*

† In Paris there are two Chief Inspectors, acting under the General Director of the administration, with twenty-five Sub-Inspectors in the various quarters of the city.

tion, the duties of the inspector are of a very responsible and delicate nature, and require strict personal attention, as may be judged from an extract taken from the Commissioner's Report:

"Placed under the immediate authority of the Prefect, the Inspector is his representative near the Boards governing the hospitals. The whole service of admission and discharge of children is entrusted to him. His office duties embrace a daily correspondence with the mayors, curates, school-teachers, and physicians; the keeping of records, and constant interviews with individuals. His labors do not cease there. By frequent and almost constant journeys only can he put the Department in intimate connection with his pupils. He must visit infant children, watch over them, and satisfy himself that they receive proper care. Is the home a healthy one? Has the child been vaccinated? Are the outfits furnished by the hospices devoted to their proper use? and, later, is the pupil surrounded by proper influences? Does he attend school, and receive proper religious instruction? Is he being prepared for the calling for which he is fitted by tastes and capacity? In a word, is the place a suitable one for him, or must another be found? These points of course require the personal examination of the inspector on the premises. With the advancing age of the children, the responsibility increases. It devolves upon him to prepare indentures of apprenticeship, to see them executed, to return some to the hospice, and to remove those who, from any cause, should not remain. His duty is also to investigate claims made by families, as well as cases of military conscription; to record the names of the children upon the census tables of the towns where they reside, and to confer with the administration upon all law questions which call for the interference of the legal guardian.

His duties do not cease towards the child until his majority or his discharge. When we consider that the supervision of the inspector involves the oversight of 5,000 pupils, more or less, who should each be visited at least once yearly; that unforeseen circumstances may, at any moment, require his presence at some distant part of the field; that nurses and patrons rarely reside in the large towns, but are scattered among little hamlets, distant from each other, which can often only be reached on foot; that sometimes, for want of nurses, children await the visit of the inspector at some distant point outside the limits of the Department, and at a great distance from the hospice intended to receive them, we must see how much zeal and active devotion are required to fulfil duties at once so varied, difficult, and delicate."

As it has been proved recently that the inspector cannot visit all his pupils yearly, and attend at the same time to other duties, sub-inspectors have in some instances been appointed, while in some other Departments Sisters of Charity and aid societies, composed of benevolent individuals, have rendered valuable service.

One of the greatest difficulties with which the General Administration of Public Charity has to contend, is in finding suitable nurses and families in the country with whom to place the children. The prices of all articles have greatly increased in France, within a few years, as well as in the United States, and it has been found necessary to increase the sum formerly allowed for the care of children. It is, however, believed that the system of temporary aid will be so economical that it will allow much more care and expense than hitherto bestowed upon those who are admitted into the public institutions, and that thereby they may be benefited both physically and morally. The prices of board hitherto paid to nurses and families have been so small, that, as a rule, only the poorer classes in the country have been willing to receive the children, and, when they have become old enough, have allowed them to live in idleness, and, in order to increase their little stipend, have permitted them to beg on the highway.

Recent investigations show, that, of the children educated in the hospice, one in five hundred and fifty-three becomes an inmate of the penitentiary, while in the whole French population there is one in six hundred and ninety-three. The proportion of females of the same class, whose names are found on the police records, is one in five hundred and eighty-two, while in the whole female population it is one in twelve hundred.

The average price of board for children of all ages until twelve is found to be six francs eighty-two centimes per month, and it is now recommended to increase this allowance, and to continue its payment until the thirteenth year, at the same time holding out every encouragement that may induce the parties to retain the child until a later period. One great object aimed at by the administration in placing children in the country, besides the principal one, the education of the child, has been to encourage agriculture, by replenishing the losses sustained by the tendency of laborers to abandon the cultivation of the fields for the great centres of trade and manufactures. The wisdom of this policy is shown by the fact that, in 1860, there were 44,000 laborers engaged in agricultural pursuits drawn from the class of foundlings alone. In most cases, the prospect of personal advantage is the only inducement for families to take charge of a pupil. Soon, however, the nurse becomes interested in her charge, and is proud of his growth and progress. As years go on, a real attachment grows up between them. All share the same privations and pleasures, and, finally, the parents know no difference between their own children and the stranger. Sometimes these families refuse to give up the child when claimed by its parents, and widows without children have been known to bequeath their property to these children. In some instances, children have been participants in the prosperity of the family, while in other instances parents have been relieved by their adopted children. It has often happened that pupils of the two sexes have married from the family which had adopted them. In one town several nurses who had received children, finding it impossible to earn their own subsistence and yet care for the children, intrusted them to the care of neighbors. The children were neglected by their attendants, and were reported to the inspector as living an idle and vagrant life. By an order of the administration they were removed, and new places found for them in a neighboring town. The removal was made without opposition, but the grief felt at the separation, though silent, was most poignant. Soon after, bitter complaints were made, and the most violent excitement shown by the nurses, who considered the children unjustly removed. The inhabitants of the neighboring town were surprised one day to see the husbands of those nurses appear with a determination at all hazards to carry off their former charges. The authorities registered the appeal, and were at a loss as to the proper mode of procedure, but sympathizing in the feelings of the men, and unwilling to sunder the ties which they themselves had been instrumental in forming, they yielded to their entreaties, and restored the children.

CHAPTER XXIX.

CHARITABLE ASSOCIATIONS.

AMONG other means of lessening the hardships of poverty are the savings banks, annuities for the aged, mutual aid associations, &c. Though these do not minister directly to the pressing wants of the poor, they are none the less useful in that they tend to promote habits of order, economy, and forethought, and thereby temperance and good morals. Other institutions may hereafter be devised, having the same objects, but in these matters great caution is necessary, as past experience sufficiently demonstrates. As an instance, it will be remembered that, during the revolution of 1848, public work-shops were established for the benefit of unemployed laborers, and that the National Assembly made an appropriation of 3,000,000 francs in their behalf. In vain was the plan opposed by some of the more prudent members of the Assembly. Mr. Thiers, in his report already quoted, said:

"An association of workmen will not prove either vigilant, or strict, or efficient, or economical, or intelligent. An employer, who cannot dismiss his workmen, award wages according to their merits, or decide summarily all questions which may arise, cannot prosper. These workmen's associations are nothing more than anarchy in industry."

The truth of these remarks was abundantly proved by the results of the experiment. The amount loaned to these associations, with interest, was 3,225,256 francs. The receipts on this amount up to Dec. 31, 1860, were 1,368,470, leaving a loss of 1,656,796. Of the whole number of fifty-six associations, only eight returned the amount of advances made. At the same time, other and wiser plans for the relief of the distressed were presented and discussed, but, from the want of practical knowledge in the Assembly, were set aside.

Another institution, founded at a still more recent period, deserves special notice. It is named in honor of the Prince Imperial, and is called *Société du Prince Imperial, Prêts de l'Enfance au travail* (loans of children to labor). Its object is, by means of a weekly assessment of two sous, voluntarily subscribed by any child in France, to loan to workmen, or individuals exercising a profession or trade, whose moral character is good, such tools, instruments, or other matters, as he may require, he agreeing to repay the loan within a certain time.*

Another institution, which has worked successfully in times of public calamity, is the Atelier de Charité, or public workshop. This organization acts as a kind of insurance for the workman in such times, and has the great advantage of giving work instead of alms, thus relieving his wants, while at the same time allowing him to retain his self-respect. These

* From a report made by Mons. Frémy to the Emperor, for the year 1865–6, it appears that, up to March 31st, the loans made amounted to 2,211,095 francs, of which 918,155 were made during the past year. The receipts were but 2,001,881 for the same period, showing a deficit of 209,213 francs.

ateliers are not of modern origin, as shown by various edicts published in 1547, 1685, 1699, 1709. The National Assembly, at the period of the Revolution, recognized their value, but finding that by their means large numbers of workmen were attracted to Paris from other countries, and that they might become an element of disorder, issued a decree on the 31st of August, 1790, of which the following are the principal provisions:

"The National Assembly, feeling how important it is that the public ateliers should be used only for the relief of those who are destitute of employment, and that the funds appropriated should be used for the greatest possible number, and, further, that they should not work to the prejudice of agriculture or manufactures, or as an encouragement to improvidence or idleness, decrees as follows: All charitable ateliers, now existing in Paris, shall be suppressed. New ateliers shall be formed in Paris or its environs, or in the Departments, when the Directors shall deem public works necessary. These ateliers shall be of two kinds. In the first, all work shall be done by the task or job. In the second, those shall be employed who have not the average strength, or those who have not been accustomed to severe manual labor.

"The price paid for the performance of the task shall be less than the current wages of the neighborhood. In Paris no one shall be admitted except he be a resident or native of the city."

A few months later an appropriation of 15,000,000 francs was made for such public works as might best meet the wants of the unemployed laboring classes, while at the same time might be useful to the country or the Department. By other acts in the following years, appropriations were made for the same object, until, in 1831, 18,000,000 were voted to be used in connection with grants by the Departments and towns, for highways and other works, on the condition, however, that said Departments and towns, before receiving any share in the grants, should vote a sum at least equal to two-thirds of the expense of the work.

These ateliers at the charge of the State, the Departments, or the towns, have now become a fixed institution, and are resorted to as the public exigency requires, especially during severe winters and times of public distress. There are some objections to the plan, as most of the work performed is on the highways, and entirely new to workmen brought up in different trades requiring little physical strength or exposure. It is of little importance what the work may be, so long as it gives temporary support and occupation to the laborers. Those who are unaccustomed to manual labor will not perhaps earn half as much as the regular laborer, as they are paid only for what they do; but they have the advantage of being kept from idleness, consequently from mischief, and what they earn seems to bridge over the days of adversity. As an instance, we may state what happened at Lyons, in 1837. Owing to stagnation of business among the silk manufacturers, many thousand laborers were thrown out of employment. Public ateliers and works on the highways were established, and the results are thus stated in a report of the authorities under whose direction the work was undertaken:

"This experiment has proved that able-bodied men can be provided for when thrown out of employment. It has given the authorities an opportunity of distinguishing the evil-disposed from the truly unfortunate, and to repress that vicious poverty which, in times of public calamity, is so apt to monopolize the means which should be used only for the benefit of the worthy poor. Finally, it has demonstrated the fact that such works can be undertaken and accomplished without hindrance or embarrassment to the regular course of industry or commerce."

Since the year 1837, similar experiments have been tried in seasons of public distress, and the results have always been satisfactory.

CHAPTER XXX.

OUT-DOOR RELIEF.

THE system of organization for the relief of the poor at their own dwellings, as well as the hospitals and hospices, is placed under the General Administration of Assistance Publique, but is managed directly by the Bureau de Bienfaisance in each arrondissement. This bureau is a central office, managed by a committee consisting of the mayor, as president, and assistants; twelve administrators, and as many visitors and Sisters of Charity as are required; a treasurer and a secretary.* There are also at-

* The number attached to each bureau depends on circumstances. The duties of these visitors consist in visiting every applicant at his own dwelling; to satisfy themselves as to his claim for assistance; to see that the sick are properly cared for, and to report all cases of admission to public institutions. They have been styled "the eyes of the administration," and the proper exercise of the duties of the office requires a good degree of judgment as well as of benevolence. Unless investigations are thoroughly and faithfully made, the whole labor is lost, and the money given worse than wasted, as it tends to encourage vice and idleness, instead of relieving the worthy poor. In a letter of instruction it is urged that "visitors should be gentle, nor ever lose their patience or *sang froid,* even when they meet with an ungracious reception, as often happens. They will avoid all manner of discussion, and will ever bear in mind that privations irritate and render unreasonable, and that the poor, to whose service we consecrate ourselves, have a claim to our indulgence and regard, even when they misinterpret our sentiments and intentions." In conjunction with the Bureaux de Bienfaisance

tached to each Bureau, surgeons, physicians, midwives (*sage femmes*), and as many employées as are found necessary for the service. The Board of Administrators correspond somewhat to our Board of Overseers of the Poor in Boston. They are nominated by the General Secretary, in concurrence with the Minister of the Interior and the Prefect of the Seine. The term of service is for three years. The Visitors* or

there are in Paris many private voluntary associations devoted to the various classes of poor and suffering; among them, La Société de la Misericorde, L'Œuvre des Faubourgs, L'Œuvre des Pauvres Maladés, La Société Philanthropique, La Société de St. Vincent de Paul, La Société Pour l'Encouragement au Bien, &c. The design of the first-named association is to search out and relieve unfortunate persons who have been reduced to poverty, after having occupied respectable positions in society, but do not ask public assistance. L'Œuvre des Faubourgs directs its efforts to the most crowded and poorest quarters, for the relief of workmen without employment, widows burdened with families, and old persons neglected by relations. L'Œuvre des Maladés and La Société Philanthropique give their attention principally to the sick at their homes. The Société de St. Vincent de Paul is a very extensive one, having branches in all parts of the world, and having many thousand members. It devotes itself principally to the sick, and to the care and instruction of children.

* The services of the physicians and surgeons were formerly gratuitous, rendering them too independent for the efficient working of the system. By a regulation of 1853 the physicians receive a salary. Those who have charge of the thickly populated quarters receive six hundred francs yearly; those who reside in the suburbs, whose districts cover a larger space, receive one thousand francs. In 1864, the number of physicians was two hundred and one. The number of sick treated by the administration at their homes in 1854 was 29,661, at an expense of 476,389 francs, or an average of 16.5 francs each. In 1861 there were 49,084 patients, at an expense of 791,449 francs. In 1864 there were 57,415 patients, at an expense of 798,276 francs. The principal items of expense of the last-named year were as follows, viz.:

Commissioners are citizens of repute, who give their services gratuitously to the work. There are also lady visitors, called dames de charité, who are chosen by the bureau in each arrondissement. The Treasurer, who also acts as Secretary, is appointed by the Prefect of the Seine, receives a salary, and gives bonds for the faithful performance of his duties. Each Bureau distributes the funds which may be appropriated to the arrondissement by the General Administration, or which may be received from private sources, and superintends such work-shops, soup depots, dispensaries, or other charitable establishments, as it may be thought desirable to maintain with-

Wages of employées, ...	63,136	francs.
Salaries of Physicians, ...	155,456	"
" of Midwives, ...	56,091	"
Support of Sisters of Charity, . .	32,475	"
Medicine and baths, ...	253,108	"
Provisions and supplies, ...	149,963	"
Money given, ...	71,108	"
" to convalescents, ...	5,042	"

Physicians are appointed for six years, by the Prefect of the Seine, on the nomination of the Bureau, and the *sages femmes*, one hundred and nine in number, in the same manner, for three years. An office is established in each quarter, where the physicians attend on stated days and administer advice and medicines. The sick confined at home are visited once each week, by one of the Commissioners or Visitors. A committee, consisting of the President or Vice-President of the Bureau, an Administrator, a physician, and the Secretary, meets once each week, to examine the reports, and to investigate all subjects pertaining to the patients. The same committee also passes upon the amount of aid to be given in common cases, but refers to the Bureau all cases seeking extra aid, as well as the claims of convalescents.

Patients are classed as acute and chronic, the last to be visited monthly. Patients may be relieved in case of emergency, at the request of the President, an Administrator, or the General Administrator, from a special fund provided for the purpose by the latter. There are now twenty Bureaux, or one for each arrondissement.

in its own sphere of operations. Each mayor presides over and superintends the Bureau of his quarter, calls and presides over meetings of his Board, and, in urgent cases, administers relief. Each year the Bureau elects a Vice-President, an Honorary Secretary, an Auditing Committee, and a delegate. The Vice-President presides in the absence of the Mayor; the Honorary Secretary conducts the correspondence and has charge of the records; and the delegate represents the Bureau at all meetings of the General Administration. The Treasurer has an office, has charge of the stores and provisions, directs the employées, and is obliged to report to the Bureau all attempts at fraud, or the adulteration of articles furnished. Physicians and surgeons with salary are attached to each Bureau, as well as midwives. Such gentlemen and lady visitors are invited to the meetings of the Bureau as may be thought desirable, and a delegate from the General Administration has the right to assist and be heard at all meetings.

During the month of May, each Bureau holds a meeting, at which are invited all the visitors, physicians, and sage femmes, who report their doings, receipts, and expenses, for the year. A report of proceedings is forwarded to the General Director. The Sisters of Charity, under the direction of the Treasurer, may distribute clothing and provisions. Services rendered in the Bureaux de Bienfaisance are classed among those which give a claim for admission to the order of the Legion of Honor. After thirty years of service, the administrators, physicians, and surgeons, may receive from the Minister of the Interior, on the recommendation of the Bureau, and with the concurrence of the General Director and Prefect, the title of Honorary Administrator or Physician.

To be entitled to aid, the applicant must have resided one year in Paris. Foreigners must have had a consecutive residence of ten years. Aid given shall be *ordinary* or *annual*, and *extraordinary* or *temporary*.

Ordinary or annual aid shall be extended to the blind, the paralytic, persons afflicted with cancer, the disabled, and those who have attained the age of sixty-four. Extraordinary or temporary aid shall be given to the wounded, the sick, women in child-bed, or nursing women having other children without means of support, foundlings, orphans, families having in charge at least three children under the age of fourteen, or two children, if one of them shall have any grave sickness, or when the wife is *enceinte* with her third child; abandoned wives, widows, or widowers, having in charge at least two children under fourteen years of age, or one child with any severe sickness or infirmity; widows or forsaken women, who, with a child under fourteen years, are *encéinte;* and finally, persons who, from any cause, find themselves reduced to extremities. No one can be aided who neglects to send his children to school, or refuses to allow them to be vaccinated.

CHAPTER XXXI.

COLONIZATION.

THE principal experiments for colonizing children have been made in Algiers. In 1852, in accordance with the recommendation of a commission composed of functionaries of the Departments of War and the Interior, two hundred children, one half taken from the foundling hospital, and the other half from poor families in Paris, were sent out, under the charge of Mons. Brummauld, and placed in the asylums of Bouffarick and Ben Ak Noun, the expenses being equally borne by government and the Department of the Seine.*

Later, eighty children, belonging to ten different Departments, were sent out in charge of Mons. P. Abram, and placed in the asylum of Minergin. Every child was to be sound in body and mind, and all were to be between ten and thirteen years of age.†

The price of board, until the age of fifteen, was eighty

* The Department of the Seine consists of the city of Paris and the villages of Sceaux and St. Denis.

† In 1860, there were eighteen colonies in the whole empire, containing but 600 pupils, and the numbers are decreasing. Of the 280 pupils received by M. Brummauld in 1852, 58 had deserted up to 1858.

centimes (sixteen cents) per day; from fifteen to eighteen, fifty centimes, when the payments ceased. At the age of twenty-one, the pupil was to receive one hundred francs, and a small grant of land. Not a long time elapsed before radical defects were found to exist in the plan adopted, and they were first pointed out by Mons. Brummauld himself, who was, more than any other person, interested in its success, and was, perhaps, better informed than any one else on the subject. In a report to the Emperor, dated July 1, 1856, he says:

"If we are enabled to say that such an education as we have given produces fruits in all the children, we must acknowledge that, destined as they are to become their own masters, the too strict routine, and minute attention to details, which we are obliged to enforce upon them all, must become onerous at a certain age. They do not learn well how to bear the burden of the day. In an institution where official superintendence takes the place of personal interest, that stimulus is wanting which in other positions is given by the necessity of earning the daily bread. Too little freedom, not enough of personal responsibility, — these are the obstacles which our young pupils have to contend with under any present organization. Many of them will not be prepared to act for themselves at twenty-one, or even at twenty-five years of age, still less to engage in any kind of business, whether of little or great importance." *

* The General Administration of Paris had formed a project of founding, for the use of that city, an institution similar to that of Mettray, but the result was too doubtful, and the expense too great. It was asked, What would Mettray have been without a Mons. Demetz?

Other objections have been urged to the plan. One writer says:

"There is an inconsistency in transporting to an unknown and foreign country, so different from their own as regards customs and climate, those hands which are in such demand at home, that in harvest time even the army has to be drawn upon in order to secure the crops. The objections urged do not apply to the experiment at Algiers alone, but the whole system is wrong in principle as well as fruitless in results. What would become of these pupils when left to themselves, without a guide or experience, and unaccustomed to act on their own responsibility? More embarrassed than pleased with their new-found liberty, exposed to temptations and the counsels of designing persons, after their little means are exhausted, would they not be tempted to engage in a career of adventure and vice, rather than in any honest labor? If we compare children educated thus with those which the General Administration has placed in families, how great will be the advantages apparent in the latter mode of education! Some similar system might be adopted for the care of vicious children, to prevent their return to the hospice, where their presence would be felt as an evil."

The difficulty in enforcing discipline and the frequency of desertions, are objections urged to the system of colonization, and have led to the general abandonment of the experiment.

It is found that the pupils dislike the confinement, and that the cost to the Department is much greater than is required by the common system in operation. In the former case, the boy is at the public charge until the age of eighteen, while in the latter he is discharged at twelve.

CHAPTER XXXII.

MONTS DE PIÉTÉ, OR PAWNERS' BANKS.

THE Monts de Piété are usually classed among public charitable institutions, and are sometimes designated as Banks for the Poor, a term which is not entirely correct, as the poor are not really the class who make the most use of them. They are, however, regarded as a most useful institution, and the influence which they have exerted in breaking up the system of usury gives them a strong claim on public gratitude, even if they exerted no other benefit. The Mont de Piété, in a great majority of cases, comes to the aid of those who cannot strictly be called *the poor*, according to the usual acceptance of the term. The embarrassed tradesman, the improvident, the gambler, the bankrupt, and even the thief, sometimes avail themselves of its benefits.

The Mont de Piété was first established in Italy to counteract the evils of usury, which had become very oppressive in that country. Barnabas de Terni, a simple monk, raised an outcry in behalf of religion against the usurious practices of the Jews, the Lombards, and their associates. Through his appeals a bank for the loan of small sums on security without interest was established at Perouse in 1462. Sums of money were loaned to persons in need, with a charge only sufficient to cover the expenses of administration. It was called *Monti di Pieta*, or Bank of Charity, a name which has been copied into French without giving the full signification of the original. The benefits conferred by the institution were so apparent that others were soon founded at Ovieto, Viterbo, Savona, Mentoni, Bologna, and other places, with the sanction of the Pope. The religious order of Recollets, who had taken the initiative in founding these establishments, were accused by the Dominicans of encouraging usury; but in spite of the opposition of this order, and the hostility of the Jews and money-lenders, the country was soon filled with similar banks. The inhabitants of many of the towns, stimulated by the example of the Recollets, established their own banks. That founded in Paris in 1493 enjoyed three centuries of prosperity. At Milan, the loans amounted to 800 ducats per month, entirely gratuitous, the surplus arising from the sale of articles pawned being distributed among the borrowers. In time, the Jews accused the banks of favoring usury secretly, while pretending to remedy the evil, and were sustained in these charges by some theologians, who quoted as authority the edicts of former Popes. The council of Latran, which began its session in 1512, under Julius II., and terminated it in 1517, under Leo X., examined the charges, and sustained the banks, on the condition that their charges on loans should not exceed the cost of administration. The council of Trent, in its seventeenth session, went still farther, and classed the Monts de Piété among the religious charitable institutions. Finally, a bank was established at Rome, in 1539, under the sanction of Pope Paul III. The by-laws were revised, in 1584, by Cardinal Borremeo, Archbishop of Milan, and under his direction it conferred great benefits on the mercantile as well as on the poorer classes. The Papal government made use of it, and princes were often glad to obtain loans on the pledge of jewels and other valuables. After a time the bank was permitted to receive the funds of private citizens on deposit, and the Jews were not backward in availing themselves of the privilege. It was then decided to pay only four per cent. on such loans, and the Jews in various ways obtained control of the sales, and held auctions, at which the articles pledged were sacrificed at the expense of borrowers. The bank at Rome attained a great degree of prosperity, making loans at two per cent. on sums exceeding thirty crowns, and gratuitously on smaller amounts. The Lombards, being driven from most European countries, found refuge in Holland, where they were tolerated, though subjected to various exactions. The outcry against them became so great, that Charles V. suppressed them in 1550, though he again tolerated them a few years later, on the condition that in no case should the rate of annual interest exceed thirty-three per cent. According to Jean Bouchet, the following rates on loans were charged by the Lombards at different periods :

From 1499 to 1515, . . .	130 per cent.	per annum.
" 1515 " 1549, . . .	$68\frac{2}{3}$ "	"
" 1549 " 1574, . . .	$43\frac{1}{3}$ "	"
" 1579 " 1593, . . .	$32\frac{1}{2}$ "	"

This statement is supposed to be somewhat exaggerated, but not very far from the truth, as the loans were usually made by the week, at exorbitant rates. Matters remained thus in Holland until the introduction of Monts de Piété, in 1610, through the exertions of an Italian named Sylvester Scarini. An architect named Coburgher afterwards founded banks in several cities on a new and simple plan. In the absence of funds of their own, the banks borrowed money of individuals at the rate of six and a quarter per cent. for six months, loaning the same at fifteen per cent. yearly, reducing the rate as the bank could afford.

The plan was to loan gratuitously to the smaller borrowers, while the larger paid interest. The institutions at Bruges and Lille made gratuitous loans. The first project for a Mont de Piété in France was submitted to Mary de Medecis, in 1611, by Hugh Delestre. It comprised a vast system of public charity and social economy, filling a quarto volume of 1400 pages. Another plan, probably by the same author, was presented to the States General in 1614, was rejected, and again taken up in 1626 by Louis XIII. The establishment of banks was authorized on certain conditions, but nothing resulted from the movement at that time. Several cities, then under foreign dominion, but now belonging to France, established banks towards the close of the fifteenth and during the sixteenth centuries. One was founded at Avignon in 1577, under the direction of Brethren of the Order of Notre Dame de Lorette, and became one of the most thriving and important of the time. Early in the reign of Louis XIV., an attempt was made to establish banks at Paris and fifty-eight other towns, on a new and singular plan. Permission was granted in 1643, and during that reign there was no other legislation, except in regard to the conditions upon which loans should be made with security. The Mont de Piété of Paris was established by a decree dated December 9, 1777. The interest on loans was fixed at ten per cent. yearly, and a small additional tax amounting to about one-half per cent. The bank was first opened in a hired building in the Rue des Blancs Manteaux, with funds loaned by the General Administration of Hospitals, who were to receive, as compensation, the profits, after deducting expenses on the sale of pledged articles. When the Revolution came, with destruction of public confidence and credit, and all its accompanying financial disasters, the Mont de Piété ceased its operations. As a relief to borrowers, the convention allowed those whose loans did not exceed twenty livres to withdraw their property from pawn, free of charge, and also passed a vote recommending the continuance of the institution. The general confiscation of the property of all charitable institutions by the Convention included that of the Bank of Paris, and after fruitless attempts at reorganization, it failed, leaving borrowers at the mercy of lenders on security. The impositions and frauds committed by the latter class became so great, as to compel the Convention to consider the propriety of reorganizing the institution, and of putting it again in operation. It was accordingly reopened in the year V, and was the subject of various legislative acts until the year XII, when it was placed upon the present basis.

By the act of June 25, 1851, it is recognized as one of the

institutions, classed as of "Utilité Publique," a technical term, carrying with it its own explanation. Monts de Piété may now be established with permission of the government, and that of the town authorities, but must be managed exclusively for the benefit of the poorer classes. The capital now employed in conducting the various institutions of this class is about 35,000,000 francs, 20,000,000 being required for the institutions of Paris alone. The principal establishment is situated in the Rue des Blancs Manteaux, with a branch in the Rue des Petits Augustins, besides seventeen smaller auxiliary offices in different quarters of the city. The number of articles received annually is 1,180,000, valued at 20,000-000 francs, 79 per cent. of which only are redeemed. 3,800 articles are deposited daily, and about 3,600 withdrawn. On Saturdays, there are usually as many as 5,000 or 6,000 articles withdrawn. In 1849, a society was formed in Paris for the purpose of redeeming from the Mont de Piété, bedding, clothing, and other articles, which have been pledged by poor people in cases of urgent necessity. It is managed by a Board, consisting of a president, vice-president, treasurer, and five lady and gentlemen counsellors.

At the end of 1853, there were forty-four Monts de Piété in France. From 1842 to 1853, inclusive, or in twenty years, they had made 20,600,226 loans, amounting to 372,-288,917 francs, or an annual average of 2,466,685 loans. The average amount of each loan was 12.57 francs; about twelve per cent. were for sums not exceeding five francs, and fifteen per cent. were for loans of five to ten francs. The loans of ten to twenty-five francs amount to eight per cent.

of the whole number, and those of twenty-five to fifty francs, to a little more than twenty-four per cent. It is thus seen that fifty-nine per cent., or about three-fifths of the capital employed, is loaned in sums of less than fifty francs. The banks at Grenoble, Toulouse, and Montpelier, loan gratuitously. That at Angers loans to the amount of five francs without interest, and charges but one per cent. for loans exceeding that sum. From 1842 to 1853, these institutions advanced 3,543,118 francs in 223,280 separate loans, which is about one per cent. of the whole amount loaned by all the institutions of the kind in France. It is thus seen that gratuitous banks loan less in proportion than those which charge interest, and this for the reason that loans of the former description are made only to persons of unquestioned moral character, while many others are prevented making application on account of the time required and necessary formalities. The remaining forty banks charged different rates of interest, varying, in 1853, from four to twelve per cent. The amounts advanced on pledged property varies in different towns, but may be generally stated thus: on silver plate and jewelry, four-fifths of the value by weight; on articles liable to depreciation, from thirty-three to eighty per cent.

From 1842 to 1853, the forty-four banks in the kingdom sold 1,920,232 articles, which realized 28,938,747 francs, or an annual average of 162,520 articles. The number of articles sold compared with the number pledged was small, showing that improvidence and vice did not induce the great mass of depositors to avail themselves of the benefits of the institution. The proportion sold, it will be seen, is only 6.58

per cent. of all articles pledged, or about one-fifteenth of the whole, during the twelve years; the average value of the articles sold was 14.83 francs. In 1853 the surplus remaining with the banks, after deducting interest, taxes, and expenses, was 640,059 francs, of which 504,274 were paid to depositors, and 135,788 remained unclaimed. It is thus seen that more than one-fifth of the amount received for sales remained unclaimed, owing to the smallness of the sum due to each depositor, which was 4.45 francs on each article. In 1853, the average rate of interest charged on loans in the various establishments was about four per cent.; six only borrowed at five per cent.; one at Luneville borrowed at six per cent. In looking at the rates of interest paid and received by the varions banks, great inequalities are noticed. Thus the banks at Boulogne, Cambrai, and Donai, borrowed at the rate of three per cent., and charged depositors twelve, — a difference of nine per cent; while at Arras, Metz, Nantes, Nismes, and Toulon, the difference was only from one to two per cent. During the year 1853, four of the establishments merely met their expenses, while the bank at Calais showed a deficit, although the rate of interest on loans was twelve per cent. The expense of management of the forty-four banks in 1853 was 1,375,546 francs, or at the rate of fifty-three centimes for each loan made. 940,670 francs were paid for salaries, and the balance, or 434,875, for rent, repairs, and general expenses.

CHAPTER XXXIII.

LA SOCIÉTÉ DU PRINCE IMPERIAL.

AN institution has lately been established in France, deserving much better the title of "Poor Man's Bank" than the Mont de Piété. It was founded by the Empress Eugenie, in 1862, and is called La Société du Prince Imperial. The best explanation of this society and its objects may be found in the Report of the Commission, addressed to the Empress, April 25, 1862. It is as follows:

MADAME, — Ever anxious to come to the assistance of the suffering, and to seek the causes of poverty, your Majesty has often been impressed in seeing the difficulty experienced by men living by their daily labor, when they are in want of a little capital for the purchase of agricultural instruments, tools, articles of prime necessity, and to meet the daily wants as they arise. You have resolved, so far as it can be done, to lessen these difficulties, by creating an institution founded upon charity. As you have witnessed the results of the efforts of the Société de la Sainte Enfance, it is your wish to follow its example in calling upon the young to assist the working-man without means; to form an association of youth, and thus constitute the Société du Prince Imperial, for the distribution of children's loans to labor (les prèts de l'enfance au travail); you have deigned to express your sentiments on this important problem of charitable economy. You have truly said, "The labor imposed upon us by God as one of our chief duties is also one of our first necessities." By labor, man increases the fertility of the soil, makes more useful and multiplies the gifts of nature. But in our state of civilization, strength and intelligence are not enough. The laborer must have animals, farming utensils; the artisan has need of tools and articles of first necessity. If the workman has no tools, the farmer no seed, the fisherman no boat; if, for the lack of a small sum of money, he cannot execute a plan, or finish what he has begun, the work is difficult, the strength flags, the ambition, will, and intelligence are paralyzed. If, however, a small loan, prudently made, permits the cultivation of the little inheritance, allows one to work steadily at the trade, to procure necessary materials, labor is resumed and misfortune is driven away. The timely advance will perhaps ensure a subsistence to an honest man, and prosperity and a good name to the family. Your Majesty attaches great importance to these loans, for the reason that they cannot be considered as alms. A loan offered to labor will exert a better and more lasting effect than a simple gift as charity. It is a mark of confidence, and tends to revive the courage, to awaken forethought, and strengthen good resolutions. Hitherto, unhappily, such loans have not been accessible to the embarrassed workman. The large capitalist cannot look after such small investments, and the smaller capitalist is too timid to make them. He dares not risk the sickness or death of the borrower; and yet the strong arms hitherto excluded from such aid, contribute essentially to the production, the increase of capital, and the prosperity of the country. You, knowing this fact, desire to afford credit to those who have none, and yet deserve it. That which single capitalists cannot do, you ask a great charitable association to perform; a society founded by yourself, and animated by such generous sentiments, with a great work to perform, will not be deterred from the work by the fear of a few losses. You will attach little importance to such risks. The poorest man may possess qualities of inestimable value, — honesty, economical habits, industry, and intelligence. These guaranties will be strengthened by timely aid, generally sufficient for the exigency, and the sum loaned will be rarely lost. Your good example, thus afforded, will show to others that men can be trusted. Private capital will then find its way more easily to the laborer's cabin and the artisan's work-shop. Great commercial advantages will thus be obtained. You have the desire that loans should be numerous, and made on the most favorable terms. To make re-payments more easy, the sum could be divided into fractional parts, and payments made at fixed times. As it is important that these loans should preserve their character, and should not be considered as a gift, it is advisable to take measures to secure their return; as there are no other guaranties than the labor and the honesty of the laborer, and of his family, there must be a real necessity for the loan, and the habits of the borrower should be laborious, and his honesty unsullied. Such is the plan, and such the object which you propose to attain, and which you have made known to us. To accomplish this end, you ask the necessary funds from private beneficence, and you found the appeal on a religious motive. It is the most prolific source of good works, for the love of God gives infinite strength to the love of our fellows. You have already created institutions for the relief of every form of misery; you have inspired pity for the most secret sufferings. It is in the name of charity you ask aid; you solicit help from all who can contribute. To give a still more prominent religious character to the enterprise, you have invited Cardinal Nicolet, archbishop of Paris, to preside over the institution. With the same object in view, you have made a loan to one of the most useful Catholic institutions, L'Œuvre de la Sainte Enfance. Taking that for a model, you would supply the treasury from gifts made by children and youth; you would thus invite all who are commencing the world, and who profit by the labor of others, while they themselves are waiting for the period when they shall engage in the serious work of life, to contribute ten centimes each week, or five francs and twenty centimes each year, to the treasury. To give an impulse to the work, which will always enjoy your powerful protection, and to exhibit in the strongest manner your interest and sympathy, your Majesty has deigned to place it under the patronage of the Prince Imperial, to the end that he may, at the same time, be a benefactor to our contemporaries, and the first member of the rising generation, which he is one day destined to govern. The participation of children in the affairs of the association will be profitable for all. For the youthful associates it will be a profitable lesson, and will give them an insight of social wants. According to your own expression, "it is the future which lends to the past" (l'avenir qui prête au passé). You invite all classes to become members of this association. To do so, requires the payment at one time of one hundred francs, and ten francs annually. This plan will permit more visits to the Savings Bank, less to the Bureaux de Bienfaisance and the hospice; will allow more money to be given to the Mutual Aid Societies, and will require the withdrawal of less."

The report is signed by the Archbishop of Paris, Messrs. Frémy, Laity, Schneider, the Duke of Bassano, and fifteen others, and is approved by the Minister of Agriculture and Commerce. The funds at the disposal of the society in April, 1864, amounted to 1,698,489 francs.

CHAPTER XXXIV.

COUNCILS DES PRUD'HOMMES.

THESE councils are instituted for the purpose of settling amicably all disputes between masters and dependents about wages, &c., in order to obviate strikes and other troubles.

By the law of 1853, the councils are composed of masters and foremen of a certain trade, elected by their associates. Masters twenty-five years of age, being French subjects of five years' standing and three years' domicil, are electors for the master Prud'hommes. Foremen and workmen under the same circumstances are electors for the foremen Prud'hommes. All electors aged thirty and upwards, knowing how to read and write, are eligible for office. The masters and foremen are equally balanced in the council, which must consist of at least six members. One-half the council is renewed every second year. The Presidents and Vice-Presidents are appointed by the Emperor, and may be selected among persons who are not eligible as members. They remain in office three years, but may be re-appointed. The different trades of Paris have been divided into four classes, viz., the metal trades, weaving, chemical preparations, and articles of Paris manufacture. These councils generally decide promptly and satisfactorily questions arising between employers and employed. Such questions relate to counterfeits, indemnities, apprenticeships, hours of labor, wages, etc. The decisions of the council are without appeal for sums not exceeding 200 francs; if above that sum, an appeal is open to the tribunal of commerce. The Emperor may dissolve the councils at any time.

TAX UPON THEATRES AND PUBLIC AMUSEMENTS.

The plan of taxing the amusements of the rich for the benefit of the poor dates back rather more than four centuries, and is one of the last remains of feudal legislation. Early attempts at dramatic representations were made under the patronage of the church, and consisted of rude representations, both sacred and profane, entitled *mysteries*, or *moralités*. The clergy were often the authors of the pieces represented, and the subjects were drawn from the Old and New Testaments. The representations were given on large platforms, erected on the public square near the church, and sometimes in the church itself, or in the cemetery, in order to give them still greater effect. In the "History of the French Theatre," we read an account of one of these representations, as follows:

"A worthy gentleman, one Nicolle de Neufchastel by name, who was curate of the Church of St. Victor de Metz, personated our Lord, and would have almost died on the cross, had he not been rescued, and another priest put in his place to represent the crucifixion for the day, and on the morrow the same curate of St. Victor performed grandly the part of the resurrection. Another priest, Monsieur Jean de Niecy, chaplain of Meltrange, personated Judas, and almost died by hanging, for his courage failed him, and he was hastily cut down and carried away."

At Angers, in August, 1486, the Dean of St. Martin personated Christ in the mystery of the Passion, while grand mass at the cathedral was performed at an earlier hour than usual, in order that the representation might be held in the same place, and also to enable the canons and choristers to be present. The first legislation on the subject of taxing public dramatic representations is found in an act of Charles VI. in 1407, approving the by-laws of a dramatic association.

By an act of Parliament, dated January 27, 1541, Charles Le Roger and his associates were permitted to represent the mysteries of the Old Testament, on the condition that they should devote one thousand livres to the use of the poor. The price of seats was fixed at two sous, and taxes for the season thirty crowns. In 1574, the curate of St. Eustache, finding that his people neglected church in order to attend the performances of the Confrères de la Passion, obtained an order that such representations should not be given until after vespers. The latter appealed to Parliament for a revocation of the order, on the plea that they had paid out three hundred livres from their receipts for divine service and the support of the poor.

In 1699, Louis XIV. levied an additional tax of one-sixth on the theatres for the benefit of the poor in hospitals.

Various changes were made from time to time in the laws regulating the tax upon public amusements, until 1817, when the act was passed which has continued in force until the present time. The theatres pay one-tenth of the gross amount received by the sale of tickets, and managers of balls, concerts, fêtes, &c., who receive money at the entrance, pay one-fourth of their gross receipts.

The amounts received during various years were as follows:

Year V of the Republic,	. 299,865	francs.
" X " " "	435,796	"
" 1810,	. 521,816	"
" 1820,	518,778	"
" 1830,	. 509,260	"
" 1840,	823,246	"
" 1864,	1,644,263	"

During the fifty years ending with 1847, from the amounts received in taxes, it is shown that the inhabitants of Paris must have expended the sum of 320,000,000 francs in public amusements.

LODGINGS.

Although the subject of lodgings does not come under the head of charities, the system adopted in the various communities, in regard to convenient distribution of room, the cost of tenements, and consequent expenses for house-rent, has much to do with the well-being of all classes.

With the completion of new streets and squares, and the wholesale destruction of buildings in Paris, entire quarters of the city have been abandoned by the working classes; and there exist the same complaints of scarcity of room and insufficiency of accommodation as in the large cities of Great Britain and the United States. These classes have been pushed into the Faubourgs; and even beyond the city walls, and the districts formerly occupied by them, have been covered with stately buildings, suited to the wants of a more elevated class of the community.

While much has been done in London, by corporations and individuals, and especially by our countryman, Mr. Peabody, little has been accomplished in Paris for the improvement of the dwellings of the working-classes. On the other hand, the accomodations furnished to those in more easy circumstances in Paris, possess various advantages, and are superior in many respects to those afforded to corresponding classes in this country. It is well known that in the large towns in France, as well as in some other countries of Europe, few families, excepting the most wealthy, occupy a separate dwelling. The houses are usually divided into flats, — one or more on each story, — in each of which are found a kitchen and other conveniences adapted to the wants and the means of the occupant. While in Edinburgh and Glasgow the same plan of lodging on flats is common, in London the system differs but little from that which prevails in this country. It is somewhat strange that a plan of living comprising so many advantages, both as regards economy and ease in housekeeping, has not been adopted by a people so eminently practical as that of New England. The economical advantages of this system are, that several families occupy the ground space devoted to one on the other plan; fewer domestics are required, and the expenses attendant upon repairs, heating, and care of halls and stairways, are divided among the tenants, thereby greatly reducing the rate of rent. On the European plan, the houses are built around the three, and sometimes the four sides of a court, with a number of the rooms facing upon it, which are thus often excluded from the sun and light. This mode of building would not generally find favor in this country, where a sunny and cheerful exposure is considered of the first importance in selecting a residence. To obviate the disadvantages of a court, while at the same time retaining the advantages of the French system, George F. Meacham, Esq., architect, of Boston, has drawn the accompanying plans, showing the front elevation, with the second and third stories of the building. The house is one hundred feet long, ninety feet deep, and contains eight different apartments.

The proposed mode of heating is by steam, and the kitchen and laundry, with their accompaniments, are removed from the main building, while light and air are abundantly secured. Ample room is furnished on the first floor and basement story for the attendants and the storage of provisions and fuel. The attic story contains extra chambers, which could be used when required by the occupants of either apartment. A few buildings, conducted partly on this plan, have been erected in this country, but generally resemble hotels rather than private residences, and have been built on expensive land, and in such a costly manner, as to present but few advantages, when regarded in an economical point of view, over the ordinary dwelling-house. It is believed that the building designed by Mr. Meacham, could be erected in a plain and substantial manner, on land of moderate cost, and that the apartments

GEO. F. MEACHAM, ARCHITECT.
23 CONGRESS ST. BOSTON.

SCALE 1/4 INCH PER FOOT.

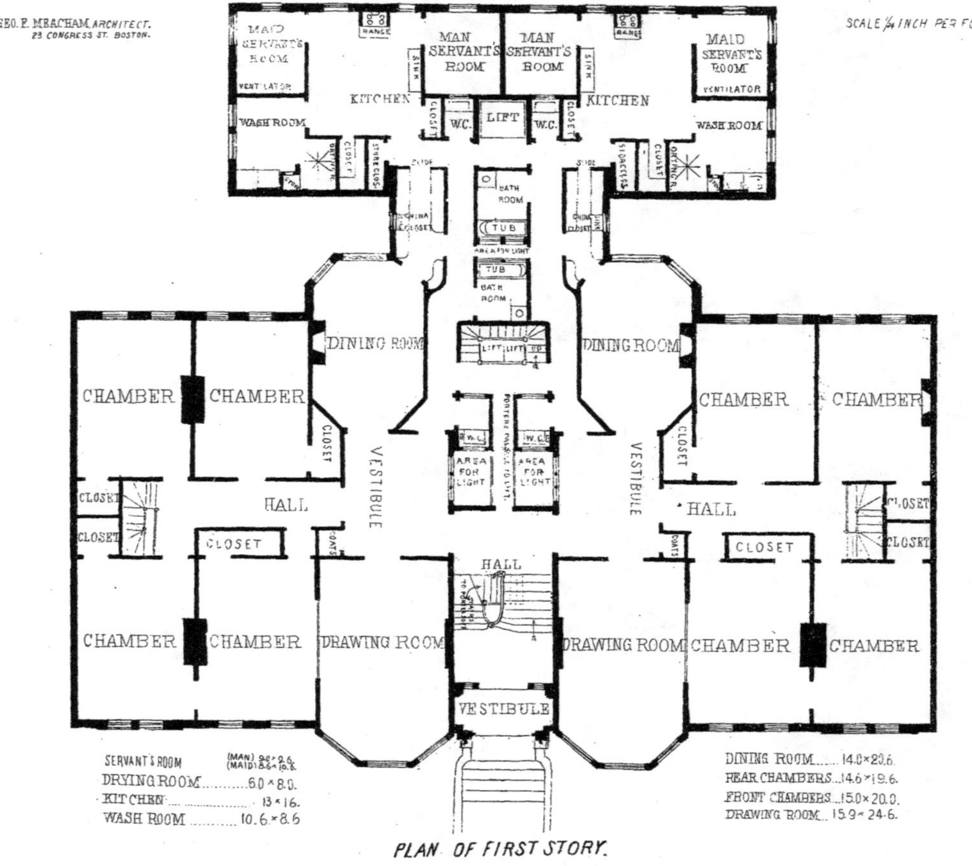

PLAN OF FIRST STORY.

GEO. F. MEACHAM, ARCHITECT.
28 CONGRESS ST. BOSTON.

SCALE 1/4 INCH PER FOOT.

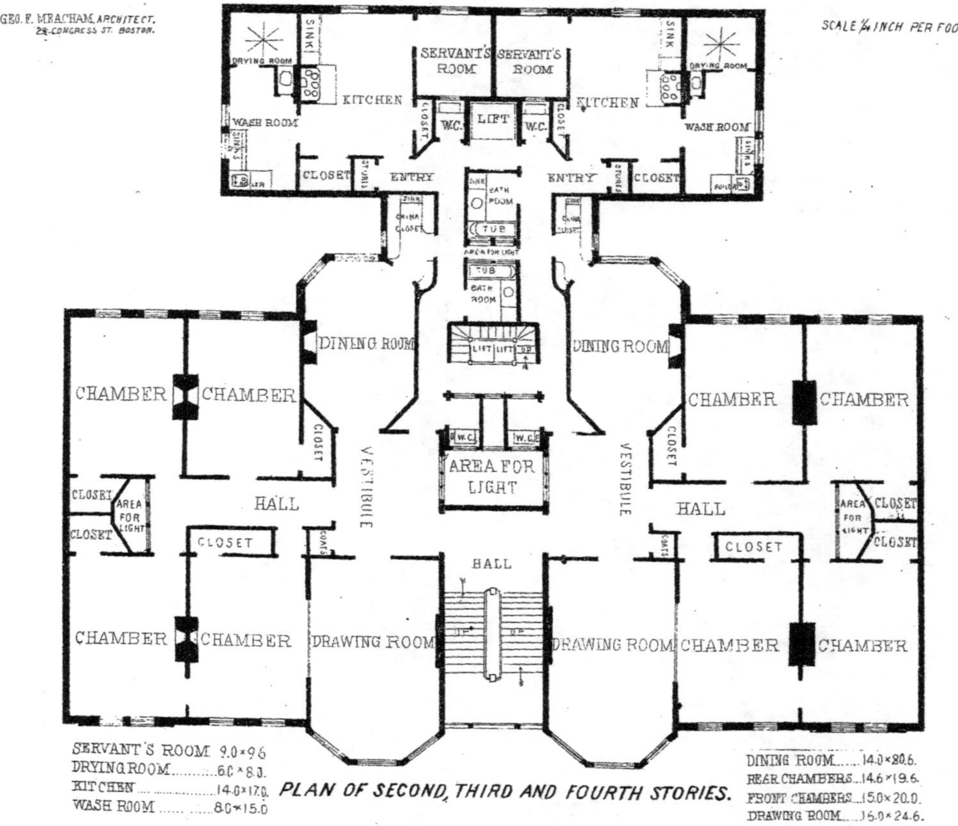

SERVANT'S ROOM 9.0×9.6
DRYING ROOM ....6.0×8.0.
KITCHEN ....14.0×17.0.
WASH ROOM ....8.0×15.0

PLAN OF SECOND, THIRD AND FOURTH STORIES.

DINING ROOM......14.0×20.6.
REAR CHAMBERS...14.6×19.6.
FRONT CHAMBERS...15.0×20.0.
DRAWING ROOM....16.0×24.6.

could be leased at a very reasonable rate, while they would at the same time be remunerative to the proprietor.

Such a building could be owned and conducted on the club system by the occupants of the various apartments, or, better still, by a capitalist, who would have the exclusive control and management of the property. We need not dwell upon the advantages of such a plan to young married people, to widows, to small families, and to any others who from taste or necessity do not wish to suffer the cares usually attending the maintenance of a separate dwelling-house.

INDEX.

INDEX.

www.ingramcontent.com/pod-product-compliance
Lightning Source LLC
LaVergne TN
LVHW011206110826
845150LV00006B/1338

* 9 7 8 1 4 2 5 5 1 8 2 2 6 *